CAREC Road Safety Engineering Manual 7

WHY AND HOW TO MANAGE SPEED

AUGUST 2024

 Creative Commons Attribution 3.0 IGO license (CC BY 3.0 IGO)

© 2024 Asian Development Bank
6 ADB Avenue, Mandaluyong City, 1550 Metro Manila, Philippines
Tel +63 2 8632 4444; Fax +63 2 8636 2444
www.adb.org

Some rights reserved. Published in 2024.

ISBN 978-92-9270-810-8 (print); 978-92-9270-811-5 (PDF); 978-92-9270-812-2 (e-book)
Publication Stock No. TIM240367-2
DOI: http://dx.doi.org/10.22617/TIM240367-2

The views expressed in this publication are those of the authors and do not necessarily reflect the views and policies of the Asian Development Bank (ADB) or its Board of Governors or the governments they represent.

ADB does not guarantee the accuracy of the data included in this publication and accepts no responsibility for any consequence of their use. The mention of specific companies or products of manufacturers does not imply that they are endorsed or recommended by ADB in preference to others of a similar nature that are not mentioned.

By making any designation of or reference to a particular territory or geographic area in this document, ADB does not intend to make any judgments as to the legal or other status of any territory or area.

This publication is available under the Creative Commons Attribution 3.0 IGO license (CC BY 3.0 IGO) https://creativecommons.org/licenses/by/3.0/igo/. By using the content of this publication, you agree to be bound by the terms of this license. For attribution, translations, adaptations, and permissions, please read the provisions and terms of use at https://www.adb.org/terms-use#openaccess.

This CC license does not apply to non-ADB copyright materials in this publication. If the material is attributed to another source, please contact the copyright owner or publisher of that source for permission to reproduce it. ADB cannot be held liable for any claims that arise as a result of your use of the material.

Please contact pubsmarketing@adb.org if you have questions or comments with respect to content, or if you wish to obtain copyright permission for your intended use that does not fall within these terms, or for permission to use the ADB logo.

Corrigenda to ADB publications may be found at http://www.adb.org/publications/corrigenda.

Notes:
In this publication, "$" refers to United States dollars.
Unless otherwise stated, the photographs in this manual were taken by Soames Job, ADB road safety consultant.
ADB recognizes "Hong Kong" as Hong Kong, China; "Turkey" as Türkiye; and "Vietnam" as Viet Nam.

Cover design by Jasper Lauzon.

Contents

Tables, Figures, and Boxes — v
Acknowledgments — vi
Abbreviations — vii
Executive Summary — viii

I. Introduction to Road Safety in CAREC Countries and the Role of Speed — 1
    A. Background — 1
    B. Purpose of This Manual — 2
    C. Global Road Safety and CAREC Road Safety — 2
    D. Safe System and Speed — 4
    E. Recommendations — 5

II. Road Design and Road Engineering — 6
    A. Setting the Right Speed Limit and Operating Speed — 11
    B. Prioritizing Road Design and Engineering Opportunities — 15
    C. Recommendations for Road Design and Engineering — 16

III. Vehicle Technology — 17
    A. Challenges of Improving Vehicle Technology — 17
    B. Vehicle Interventions to Help Limit Speed — 17
    C. Prioritizing Vehicle Technology Opportunities — 20
    D. Recommendations for Vehicle Technology — 20

IV. Changing Road-User Behavior — 21
    A. Enforcement and Communications — 21
    B. Maximising the Benefits of Enforcement and the Power of General Deterrence — 25
    C. What Works in Behavior Change — 27
    D. Prioritizing Behavior Change Opportunities — 32

V. Reducing Speed Through Modal Shift and City Planning — 33
    A. Modal Shift — 33
    B. Urban Planning — 34
    C. Prioritizing Modal Shift and City Planning Opportunities — 35

VI. Delivering Improved Speed Management: Persuading and Managing Delivery of What Works — 37
    A. Selecting the Best Speed Management Actions — 37
    B. Managing and Delivering Implementation — 43

VII. Evidence for the Role of Speed in Crashes: Dispelling Myths and Misinformation 45
    A. The Contribution of Speed to Crashes and Their Severity 45
    B. The Contributions of Speed to Crash Trauma 47
    C. Economic Costs of Crash Deaths and Injuries 50
    D. The Known Effects of Speed Apply in CAREC Countries 53
    E. Common Myths About Speed 57
    F. Recommendations 61

Appendixes

1 Examples of Private Sector Campaigns Encouraging Speed 63

2 Why Driver and School Education Is Ineffective 65

Tables, Figures, and Boxes

TABLES

1	Comparison of Atlanta, United States and Barcelona, Spain	35
2	Assessment of Interventions for Managing Speed in CAREC Countries	40
3	Speed Limits and Potential Savings of Fatalities in CAREC Countries	41
4	Cost of Crashes Each Year in CAREC Countries	51
5	Features of CAREC Countries That Demonstrate Importance of Speed Reduction	54
6	Pedestrians in Crash Deaths in CAREC Countries	55

FIGURES

1	Relationship Between Enforcement Increases and Crash Decreases	21
2	Processes Necessary for General Deterrence and Behavior Change in Road Safety	26
3	The Graduated Licensing System from New South Wales, Australia	31
4	Benefit-Cost Ratios for Selected Interventions for Speed Management	39
5	Relationship Between the Rate of Drivers Yielding to Pedestrians and Approach Speed	46
6	Small Changes in Speed Have Large Impacts on Road Crash Deaths and Injuries	47
7	Risk of Death by Speed of Impact for Different Crash Types	49
8	Impact of Changes in Speed on Components of Travel Cost in Iran	51
9	Relationship Between Speed and Traffic Flow	58

BOXES

1	Business and Economic Benefits of a 30-Kilometer Per Hour Zone in Shanghai	13
2	The Introduction of Regulations for Speed Managing Technology in the European Union	19
3	Good Practice in Automated Speed Enforcement in Mongolia	29
4	Case Studies of Bus Rapid Transit Developments in the People's Republic of China and Pakistan	34

Acknowledgments

This manual was prepared under an Asian Development Bank (ADB) technical assistance grant, TA-6591 REG: Enhancing Road Safety for Central Asia Regional Economic Cooperation (CAREC) Member Countries (Phase 2). Its production was administered and managed by the road safety and CAREC Secretariat teams at ADB, Ritu Mishra, Pilar Sahilan, and David Shelton. Valuable inputs on the manual were provided by CAREC governments, David Cliff (Global Road Safety Partnership), and Greg Smith (International Road Assessment Programme).

Soames Job, ADB consultant, is the author of this manual.

Abbreviations

BCR	–	benefit–cost ratio
BRT	–	bus rapid transport
CAREC	–	Central Asia Regional Economic Cooperation (Program)
ESC	–	electronic stability control
GDP	–	gross domestic product
GLS	–	graduated licensing scheme
GPS	–	global positioning system
HIC	–	high-income country
iRAP	–	International Road Assessment Programme
ISA	–	intelligent speed adaptation or assessment
km/h	–	kilometers per hour
LMICs	–	low- and middle-income countries
mm	–	millimeter
NGO	–	nongovernment organization
NSW	–	New South Wales
PRC	–	People's Republic of China
UN	–	United Nations
UNESCAP	–	United Nations Economic and Social Commission for Asia and the Pacific
US	–	United States

Executive Summary

Managing speed is one of the most powerful and cost-effective ways to achieve road safety. It has the potential to reduce crash frequency and severity, as well as to deliver many other direct economic and social benefits. Despite this, the practice of speed management remains underestimated, poorly understood, and inadequately addressed around the world. This manual works toward correcting this by perusing evidence on the benefits of safe speed. While the manual does not suggest lowering speeds to a point restricting mobility, lowering speeds from extremely high levels to lower but still high levels is ultimately not enough. This manual instead promotes working toward "safe system" speeds.

This manual provides a summary of evidence to guide improved speed management across multiple areas of opportunity in Central Asia Regional Economic Cooperation (CAREC) countries. A selection of specific speed management interventions are canvased and prioritized. A business case for speed management is presented. The manual also addresses common misunderstandings and prevalent misinformation to guide communications with the public and informal discussions with decision-makers, partners, and stakeholders.

Each element of any road transport system—roads and roadsides, vehicles, speeds, human behavior—can be improved to create the most cost-effective, appropriate path to delivering safety. Evaluations show that the high cost-effectiveness of speed management interventions often warrants a focus on speed to improve road safety, especially where road safety resources are constrained.

The manual comprises the following modules:

I. Introduction to Road Safety in CAREC Countries and the Role of Speed. The evidence for the critical role of speed in crashes fully applies in CAREC countries largely because the universal laws of physics determine the effects of speed. Crashes on average cost 4.6% of gross domestic product in CAREC countries each year, higher than the global average for middle-income countries. Noting that crash data consistently underestimate speeding as a factor in fatal crashes, speeding crashes contribute more than half this cost (over 2.3% of gross domestic product). This is an avoidable burden of speeding on CAREC economies.

II. Road Design and Engineering. This module describes the evidence-based opportunities for road safety improvements via highly effective features that help to manage speeds (often referred to as traffic calming), such as speed humps, raised platforms, chicanes, roundabouts, lane narrowing, and gateway treatments. Speed limits are also critical and must be set with a focus on safety risks, including protecting vulnerable road users on roads where they are present. Best practice has steadily shifted in good road safety countries from 50 kilometers per hour (km/h) to 40 km/h for urban roads with 30 km/h limits in pedestrian areas.

III. Vehicle Technology. This module provides the evidence base for effective speed managing interventions in vehicle technology. Technologies that force speeds down (such as those that limit the speed of a vehicle) are the most powerful. However, the European Union mandate for intelligent speed adaptation offers more immediate opportunities through adoption of similar regulations.

IV. Changing Road-User Behavior. Many commonly held views of how to best achieve behavior change are not effective. Evidence shows what works for speed management, and highlights the importance of general deterrence and the interventions that deliver this. Various speed enforcement methods, as well as well-designed enforcement- rather than crash-risk-based campaigns, are effective.

V. Reducing Speed Through Modal Shift and City Planning. Effective land-use policy and city planning can help reduce speed, as well as road travel demand. Road safety must engage with these arenas to reduce the need for road travel and reduce the motivation to speed.

VI. Delivering Improved Speed Management: Persuading and Managing Delivery of What Works in Speed Management. Speed-managing interventions achieve impressively high benefit-to-cost ratios, which are often higher in lower-to-middle-income countries than in high-income countries. This module provides guidance on delivering speed-reducing interventions and policies, processes for selecting the best opportunities for each country, and steps for implementation. Suggestions are offered for persuading key decision-makers, politicians, stakeholders, and delivery partners of the need to manage speed effectively.

VII. The Evidence for the Role of Speed in Crashes: Dispelling Myths and Misinformation. Speed plays a powerful role in both crash occurrence and severity, but many common views on speed and speed management are erroneous. In addition to the trauma and costs of speeding crashes, speed-related but non-speeding crashes, which occur where speed limits are too high for safety, add to this burden. Evidence shows that contrary to common belief, lower speeds generally improve national economies and increase long-term economic growth. This is because safe speeds reduce the large economic costs of crash deaths and injuries as well as other areas of economic loss. These costs exceed the costs of slower travel. While travel time savings are important, transport policy must shift from a singular focus on travel time savings to include the many areas of economic costs of speed.

Conclusion. The costly impacts of speed can be effectively managed by adopting evidence-based interventions to deliver safe speeds. Interventions that reduce speed are a cost-effective opportunity for CAREC countries to dramatically reduce crash deaths and injuries within a reasonable time frame. Speed-managing interventions are highly cost effective, with some returning $17 in savings for every $1 invested. CAREC governments will find it challenging to find investments with stronger returns than these.

Reducing travel speeds by just 10 km/h across all roads in the CAREC region would result in a reduction in the number of crash deaths to less than half current levels and deliver additional economic benefits. A broad adoption of multiple powerful speed reducing interventions is critical for road safety and for other social and economic benefits. The business case is compelling for CAREC member countries to adopt speeds that protect pedestrians and other vulnerable road users, and to move beyond the misinformation that has constrained speed management policy all over the world.

I. Introduction to Road Safety in CAREC Countries and the Role of Speed

A. Background

Central Asia Regional Economic Cooperation (CAREC) countries committed to road safety at the 14th CAREC Ministerial Conference in 2015. In 2016, the *CAREC Road Safety Strategy 2017–2030* was endorsed by CAREC ministers at the 15th Ministerial Conference. The strategy supports and encourages governments and road authorities to plan, design, construct, operate, manage, and maintain roads with road safety as a key and specific objective. In addition, in 2022 the United Nations (UN) Economic and Social Commission for Asia and the Pacific (UNESCAP) released a road safety strategy for Asia and the Pacific agreed by the countries of the region.[1] This manual also aligns with and supports the Global Plan for the Decade of Action 2021–2030, its associated targets, and the UN Sustainable Development Goals.[2]

In support of road safety in CAREC countries, the Asian Development Bank (ADB) is developing the *CAREC Road Safety Engineering Manuals*. This manual is the seventh in the series. The others cover road safety audits, safer road works, roadside hazard management, pedestrian safety, star ratings for road safety audits, and blackspots. These touch on aspects of speed management, which particularly relate to Module II (Road Design and Engineering) in this manual.

The role of speed in both road crashes and crash severity is deeply underestimated. The effective management of speed to levels where people will not die or be seriously injured in crashes delivers a profound set of benefits beyond road safety; it is one of the most powerful and cost-effective mechanisms by which crash deaths can be prevented and disabilities avoided in CAREC countries. Evidence shows that speed reductions across the CAREC region of just 10 kilometers per hour (km/h) would more than halve crash deaths. In addition, lower speeds would deliver improved national economic growth.

Despite the evidence for deaths and injuries being dramatically reduced, no CAREC country currently has good-practice speed limits or speed management in place, both of which are fundamental to the safe system approach. A safe system is one that follows a guiding philosophy based on the principles that humans inevitably make mistakes and that they are vulnerable to crash forces. Such a system aims to protect people from death and serious injury through roads, vehicles, and speeds that limit crash forces to survivable levels.[3] The implementation of evidence-based policies and action by the governments of CAREC countries are required to achieve national benefits.

Speed management is the greatest road safety opportunity available to CAREC (and many other) countries, yet speed management is the most underestimated, poorly understood, inadequately addressed, and resisted opportunity on the basis of misinformation. This manual works toward correcting this situation by providing relevant scientific evidence and showing the many unexpected benefits of interventions to reduce speeds.

---

[1] S. Job. 2022. Regional Plan for Asia and the Pacific: The Second Decade of Action for Road Safety. Bangkok: United Nations Economic and Social Commission for Asia and the Pacific (UNESCAP).

[2] World Health Organization (WHO) and the United Nations Regional Commissions. 2021. Global Plan for the Decade of Action for Road Safety 2021–2030. Geneva: WHO.

[3] R.F.S. Job, J. Truong, and C. Sakashita. 2022. The Ultimate Safe System: Redefining the Safe System Approach for Road Safety. *Sustainability*. 14 (5).

B. Purpose of This Manual

This manual provides guidance for CAREC countries on how to achieve improved speed management, and why it is worth achieving. It provides a practical point of reference for improving speed management and may be used as a basis for relevant training, advocacy support, and to set out the business case for speed management interventions. The manual also serves to expand an understanding of the importance of reducing speed in road safety, and provides a guide for necessary evidence-based actions by stakeholders. The policies and actions in this manual are recommended for all CAREC countries, all stakeholders, and all levels of government.

Evidence is presented to provide a basis for the development of business cases for speed management relevant to all stakeholders. The manual is structured to speak as well to specific stakeholders, highlighting the benefits across many agenda, not only safety, from managing speed:

- **Policymakers, legislators, funding decision-makers, and road-safety managers.** A delivery framework, with planning for delivery, resourcing, monitoring, management, and continuous improvement of safe speed is presented.
- **Road safety engineers, designers, operators, and auditors.** Safe speed through road design and road safety engineering is covered.
- **Vehicle engineers, vehicle standards policymakers, and enforcement officers.** Safe speed through vehicle features and their maintenance is discussed.
- **Traffic police, enforcement officers, those setting penalties, and communications and marketing experts.** Creating general deterrence to effectively reduce speeding is covered.
- **Driver trainers and road safety educators.** Elements shown to be effective for road safety are presented.
- **The private sector and its regulators.** Opportunities for private sector contributions to road safety and the need for government regulation to achieve these are also discussed.

C. Global Road Safety and CAREC Road Safety

Saving lives and avoiding injuries suffered through road crashes are more urgent goals than ever before in the CAREC region, and the Asia and Pacific region more broadly. We now know that road crashes not only bring deaths, injuries, permanent disabilities, grief, and suffering, but also lead to family poverty, create substantial economic costs for countries, and retard long-term national economic growth.

The cost of crash deaths and injuries averages 4.6% of gross domestic product (GDP) each year in CAREC countries. More than half of this cost is caused by speeding, highlighting the vital need to improve speed management in CAREC countries.[4]

Globally, around 1.3 million people die in road crashes each year.[5] In addition, many millions are seriously injured. Over 90% of deaths occur in low- and middle-income countries (LMICs), regularly devastating families, driving many into poverty, and harming national economies. Road safety particularly impacts the most vulnerable members of society. Most road crash victims are males, but the economic hardships this creates greatly affect women and families. The inability of many countries to provide accurate data about the number of people seriously injured in crashes is itself an additional barrier to improving road safety.

On 31 August 2020, the UN General Assembly proclaimed 2021–2030 as the Second Decade of Action for Road Safety, with a goal of reducing road crash deaths and injuries by at least 50% between 2021 and 2030.[6]

A powerful global push for road safety continues. The UN's 2030 Agenda for Sustainable Development includes two targets related to road safety:

- **Sustainable Development Goal 3.6 (health):** By 2030, halve the number of global deaths and injuries from road traffic crashes.

---

[4] Calculated using updated data following the methods of W. Wambulwa and R.F.S. Job in Guide for Road Safety Opportunities and Challenges: Low and Middle Income Country Profiles. 2019. Washington, DC: World Bank.
[5] WHO. 2018. Global Status Report on Road Safety. Geneva.
[6] Via adopting Resolution 74/299.

- **Sustainable Development Goal 11.2 (cities).** By 2030, provide access to safe, affordable, accessible, and sustainable transport systems for all, improving road safety, notably by expanding public transport, with special attention to the needs of those in vulnerable situations, women, children, persons with disabilities, and older persons.

The recommended actions in this manual also directly support CAREC countries in delivering on three of the agreed World Health Organization (WHO) Global Road Safety Performance Targets:

- Target 3: By 2030, all new roads achieve technical standards for all road users that take into account road safety, or meet a three-star rating or better. (Safe speeds improve road safety star ratings.)
- Target 4: By 2030, more than 75% of travel on existing roads is on roads that meet technical standards for all road users that take into account road safety. (Safer speeds support this because at lower speeds, the technical requirements for safety are less demanding.)
- Target 6: By 2030, halve the proportion of vehicles traveling over the posted speed limit and achieve a reduction in speed-related injuries and fatalities. (Most of the manual supports this.)

The Road Safety Imperative for CAREC Countries

The UN Sustainable Development Goal of halving deaths due to road crashes and injuries by 2030 is achievable for CAREC countries, with improved management of speed being crucial. Meeting this target will deliver profound reductions in human suffering, grief, and economic costs. This manual, and other CAREC road safety manuals, help CAREC countries to hit that target.

CAREC countries face the added challenge of motorization rates increasing from a relatively low base, meaning that the road safety risk is escalating due to rising exposure. CAREC countries average 168 passenger vehicles per 1,000 people, placing them above the average for Asia (excluding the high-income countries [HICs] of Japan, the Republic of Korea, and those in the Middle East), but well below the HICs of Europe and North America.[7]

Before considering the evidence relating speed to crashes, there is a need to consider the applicability of the evidence to CAREC countries. CAREC countries face greatly varying road safety challenges, including large, high-density cities with trucks, cars, motorcycles, bicycles, and pedestrians all mixing on the roads, remote mountainous roads, and modern freeways. In some CAREC countries, motorcycles are a substantial share of the cause of traffic and deaths, while in others they are rare.

Road safety is improved through adoption of actions for which there is clear evidence of success. Without evidence, policy and practice are informed only by peoples' beliefs, views, and supposed common sense—but this is a recipe for failure.

> *In improving road safety, choosing actions based on "common sense" or personal experience rather than evidence is a recipe for failure.*

Road safety actions must be chosen based on the evidence for what works. Much evidence comes from non-CAREC areas. Despite the distinct features of the CAREC region, it still has much in common with the rest of the world when it comes to road safety. Critical shared factors include:

(i) the universal applicability of the laws of physics, which make speed the fundamental determinant of both crash risk and severity;
(ii) the inevitability of human error;
(iii) the limitations of the human body to survive forceful impacts; and
(iv) the psychology of human judgement of risk.

Two responses are most commonly formulated on the issue of applicability and learning from other countries:

(i) "My country is different and so the evidence does not apply."
(ii) "The scientific evidence applies the same way everywhere."

---

[7] Based on data from the International Organization of Motor Vehicle Manufacturers (Organisation Internationale des Constructeurs d'Automobiles).

Both impede progress in road safety. Some evidence will apply, and some will not. The art is in determining which applies. Examples provide a good guide to determining what will apply. To illustrate, barriers that separate traffic moving in opposite directions will prevent head-on crashes in any country, and the human tendency to stop a certain behavior, such as speeding, when facing punishment is common across all countries. However, the level of penalty that will deter unsafe behavior will differ from country to country, and the messages that best promote the effectiveness of enforcement may vary across cultures. Thus, while this manual recommends established successful principles for messages and campaigns, it does not recommend any specific way of presenting a message based on successes in other countries.

Most importantly, reducing speed will create road safety benefits everywhere because of the basic laws of physics. Properly designed speed humps, raised platforms, and other road features will slow average travel speed and reduce speeding in any country, as will the right penalties and level of enforcement speeding. The evidence on these interventions is directly applicable in CAREC countries, noting that road safety in LMICs is especially sensitive to speed, and that speed-managing actions often yield much higher benefit–cost ratios (BCRs) in LMICs than HICs.

D. Safe System and Speed

The "safe system" approach recognizes that road transport is a complex system and places safety at its core. In essence, a safe system recognizes that humans, vehicles, and road infrastructure must interact in a way that ensures a high level of safety.

A safe system:

- accepts that human error is inevitable and accommodates errors;
- incorporates road and vehicle designs that limit crash forces to levels that are survivable and do not cause serious injury;
- motivates those who design and maintain roads, manufacture vehicles, and administer safety programs to accept and address shared responsibility for safety, so that when a crash occurs, systemic remedies are found rather than the driver or other road users being blamed;
- pursues a commitment to proactive and continuous improvement of roads and vehicles so that the entire system is made safer, rather than just locations or situations where crashes have occurred; and
- adheres to the underlying premises that the transport system should produce zero deaths and zero serious injuries, and that safety should not be compromised for the sake of other factors such as cost or faster transport times.[8]

A safe system can be achieved by either (i) creating a road environment in which the crash type is physically impossible (e.g., median barriers prevent head-on crashes and well-designed roundabouts prevent side impact crashes); or (ii) managing speeds down to levels at which the crash type is survivable. Elements of the system—speed, roads and roadsides, vehicles—can each be improved to different degrees to create the most cost-effective, appropriate path to delivering a safe system. In the case of vulnerable road users, road engineering solutions are less feasible, and lower speeds are required. Speed is most fundamental to a safe system, because in addition to contributing to crash occurrence, it is a major determinant of the level of crash force that must be managed to allow crash survivability.[9]

Safe speeds are, by convention, set at a point that will allow a 90% survival rate in crashes at that speed. These already represent a compromise because some deaths will still occur, though will be greatly reduced; they represent a trade-off with mobility.[10]

These speeds are:

- 30 km/h for impacts with pedestrians (and other vulnerable road users such as bicyclists),
- 40 km/h for impacts with fixed objects,

---

[8] WHO and the United Nations Regional Commissions. 2021. *Global Plan for the Decade of Action for Road Safety 2021–2030*. Geneva: WHO; and also incorporates the revised position on shared responsibility in R.F.S. Job, J. Truong, and C. Sakashita. 2022. *The Ultimate Safe System: Redefining the Safe System Approach for Road Safety*. *Sustainability*. 14 (5).

[9] International Transport Forum (ITF). 2022. Road Safety. *Implementing the Safe System*. Paris.

[10] For a safe system, these speeds are the maximum travel speeds that should be allowed, not design speeds or average speeds.

- 50 km/h for car-to-car direct side impact crashes, and
- 70 km/h for head-on crashes.

The practical consequences of speeds above these safe system speeds are critical. For example, a pedestrian hit at 30 km/h has a 90% chance of survival, but at 50 km/h, the same pedestrian has little chance of survival.[11]

These speeds apply to fatal crash outcomes. To also avoid serious injury, speeds need to be lower than those identified above. A more recent analysis of speed and fatal crash risk indicates that the impact speed at which 10% of pedestrians will die is higher than 30 km/h, at around 37 km/h. At the same time, another recent analysis of speed and serious injury risk indicates the need for lower speeds, especially for pedestrians, for whom 10% will be seriously injured at an impact speed of only 20 km/h.[12]

The World Bank Global Road Safety Facility has made evidence-based estimates of the dramatic road safety benefits of LMICs lowering all speeds to safe system speeds. These analyses reveal reductions in fatalities of 30% for urban roads, 24.5% for rural roads, and 19.7% for motorways.[13] No other methods for improving road safety can feasibly compete with the cost of lowering speeds and the time frame in which this can be achieved. Based on the low proportion of motorway deaths compared with urban and rural deaths, these reductions will deliver over half the UN target of a 50% reduction in deaths by 2030.

As an example of other options available, where car-to-car direct side impact crashes can occur, speeds can be limited to 50 km/h, or the location can be redesigned to avoid direct side impact crashes (e.g., through a roundabout), or the protection afforded by the sides of vehicles can be improved.

E. Recommendations

Some recommendations include the following:

- Consider the large human, social, and economic costs being borne by CAREC countries through road crashes.
- Consider the speeds identified in the safe system approach to road safety as a guide to the speeds required for safety in various road locations.

---

[11] See "The effects of impact speed on the chances of surviving a crash," in Module VII, for details of evidence.
[12] C. Jurewicz et al. 2016. Exploration of Vehicle Impact Speed–Injury Severity Relationships for Application in Safer Road Design. *Transportation Research Procedia*. 14. pp. 4247–4256.
[13] L. W. Mbugua et al. 2021. Potential Reductions in Road Fatalities and Injuries from Reducing Speed Limits to Recommended Safe System Speed Limits in Low- and Middle-Income Countries. (Preprint.)

II. Road Design and Road Engineering

Managers of road and traffic networks who are responsible for the safety of road users have several tools available to them to manage safe speeds. One is this series of manuals, which provides guidance on critical road safety engineering topics, each one of which interacts with the issue of safe speeds. Safe speeds, compliant within safe systems, should be high on the list of considerations for designers and auditors. *CAREC Road Safety Engineering Manual 1: Road Safety Audit* outlines the audit process, and guides auditors toward considering ways to safely manage speeds. Safe speeds through road work zones are addressed in *CAREC Road Safety Engineering Manual 2: Safer Road Works*.

As impact speeds are critical within safe systems to minimize the risk of fatal and serious casualty outcomes, and as run-off-road crashes as well as pedestrian crashes tend to be overrepresented in speed-related crashes, two other CAREC manuals also interact with this topic. *CAREC Road Safety Engineering Manual 3: Roadside Hazard Management* provides guidance on how to reduce this large group of collisions, while *CAREC Road Safety Engineering Manual 4: Pedestrian Safety* guides designers and managers on ways to reduce collisions involving this vulnerable group of road users.

The physical road environment, including road design, infrastructure, and the highway engineering that regulates the movement of traffic, offers important opportunities to manage speeds. Effective interventions using national road rules, road design, and engineering measures offer sustainable, effective, and continuous (24 hours per day, 7 days per week) management of speeds. These interventions may be applied in urban or rural environments, on low- or high-speed roads. While each may serve slightly different purposes, all are essential for effective speed management at the national level. When used in combination, maximum safe speed management can be achieved. *CAREC Road Safety Engineering Manual 5: Star Ratings for Road Safety Audit* brings together the consideration of safe speeds in designs and audits as one step toward achieving a higher star rating (or safety rating) for a new or rehabilitated road. The manuals are a resource to assist, inform, and guide professionals to manage safer speeds and safer roads for all across the CAREC region.

Road authorities can apply three broad categories of engineering measures, singly or in combination, to manage and control vehicle speeds.

1. National default speed limits. Most countries have a maximum speed limit for rural roads and another, usually lower, speed limit for urban roads, for locations where no speed restriction signs are in place—these are sometimes referred to as default speed limits. In most CAREC countries, there is a default 90 km/h speed limit on rural roads, while on urban roads, the default speed limit is 60 km/h. Having such limits within the national road rules can be useful to provide an overarching regulation for speeds on all roads, without the need for speed restriction signs to be installed. However, default speed limits can also constrain sound management of speed for safety.

Default speed limits are low cost, but they are insensitive for three reasons:

(i) Some roads, particularly in rural areas with confined horizontal and vertical alignments, warrant a lower speed limit than the national default, and drivers who blindly believe the default speed in such environments is safe may suffer from this error. Such roads usually need to have speed signs installed to override the default limit. Equally, urban areas may have narrow roads where a default of 60 km/h is clearly too high for safety, so relying on the default speed limit can be high risk.

(ii) Drivers and riders must know when they are on an urban as opposed to rural road. Some situations will not be clear. For instance, across the CAREC region, buildings may be beside roads but outside designated (signed) village areas; to some drivers these buildings indicate an urban area, to others they do not. Unless regulatory speed restriction signs are installed to override the national default limit, disagreements may occur between drivers and riders and traffic police.

(iii) Default speed limits are insensitive to the risks of vulnerable road users, especially pedestrians, who are at high risk in CAREC and countries, in Asia and the Pacific generally, and are best protected through lower vehicle speeds.

Therefore, while it may be useful to have default speed limits written into national road rules, the road authority responsible for managing speed zones must have the power to set limits below default speeds and should be alert to the need to add speed restriction signs to sections of roads that are open to differing interpretations, and those that demand lower speed limits, especially due to the presence of vulnerable road users. For safety, the national highway authority should review its default speed limits and consider lowering them in line with safe system speeds. For instance, a 60 km/h urban default speed limit is no longer considered safe or appropriate in countries with good road safety records. Instead, default urban limits of 40 km/h or 50 km/h are now common. Similarly, as many rural roads do not allow for safe travel at the default speed limit, many more regulatory speed restriction signs should be used. The default speed limit continues to be a necessary feature of speed management but is gradually being overtaken by the widespread installation of regulatory speed restriction signs.

2. Regulatory speed restriction signs. These are signs that display the maximum speed limit for the road ahead to approaching drivers and riders. Regulatory speed restriction signs may be used to supplement the national default speed limit but are more often used in locations where the default limit would be too high for the conditions. What defines a speed limit should be stated in the national road rules, but in general it is created when a regulatory speed restriction sign is posted at the beginning of a zone, and another speed restriction sign is placed at the end. The length of the zone may be 500 meters (it is not considered good practice to have speed zones shorter than this for enforcement reasons), or it may be many kilometers. When a speed zone becomes quite long, it is good practice to repeat speed restriction signs at agreed spacings along the zone. For two-way roads, the same speed limit should apply in both directions and be signed similarly in each direction.

Regulatory speed restriction signs are an important form of traffic control. They require compliance from drivers and riders, and to achieve this, they should be installed consistently across the road network. As well, they require consistent enforcement by traffic police.

Permanent regulatory speed restriction signs should not be installed alongside warning signs to alert drivers and riders of a hazard ahead. Too often in CAREC countries, they are seen with warning signs for bridges, pedestrian crossings, and curves. They often display quite low speed values and while they do commence a speed zone, the absence of another speed restriction sign beyond the hazard means that the speed limit continues indefinitely. Such open-ended speed zoning undermines the value and usefulness of these important regulatory signs.

The default national speed limit applies when there are no regulatory speed restriction signs installed (photo by Phil Jordan).

Regulatory speed restriction signs may also be used for temporary use such as at road works or where an emergency situation demands traffic to slow (photo by Phil Jordan).

In situations where road users need to negotiate a hazard at a reduced speed, advisory speed plates may be attached to the warning sign. Advisory speed plates are not enforceable, but they offer practical safety advice to drivers and/or riders.

Temporary speed restriction signs are used at road works, on managed expressways (which have incident management or congestion management capabilities controlled from a traffic control center), or at scenes of local emergencies, such as major collisions or weather impacted and damaged roads. The signs used at road works, or in emergency situations, should be regulatory signs and these may be used on tripods, in multi-message frames, or placed on posts. They may be needed for less than a day or up to several months, depending on the situation. Details of signs needed for safe road works are provided in *CAREC Road Safety Engineering Manual 2: Safer Road Works*.

When setting speed limits and overseeing the installation of permanent or temporary regulatory speed restriction signs, several issues should be considered:

- **The number of signs used to inform drivers and riders of a change of speed zone, and then the number of signs used to remind them of the new limit.** Often a single sign is installed on the same side of the road that driving takes place, but there is growing awareness of the benefits of installing a pair of duplicate signs on national highways, especially on dual carriageway roads. Pairs of signs increase their conspicuousness and minimize the risk of a driver or rider missing them.
- **The size and placement of each speed restriction sign, which should comply with national guidelines.** In general, sign sizes range from regular (typically 450 x 600 millimeters [mm]), to medium (600 x 900 mm) to large (900 x 1200 mm). Larger signs should be used in locations with high approach speeds, or where there is a greater need for sign prominence due to competing visual stimuli. The larger size is common on high-speed roads such as expressways, while regular size is commonly used on most urban roads. All signs used on CAREC roads, including regulatory speed restriction signs, should be conspicuous to approaching road users.
- **The speed value on the sign, which should conform to the national speed management policy and guidelines, if they exist.** A national committee comprising the road authority, traffic police, and other key stakeholders should develop a speed management strategy that contains, among other things, the agreed speed limit values for the country. These limits should conform to safe system speeds.
- **Traffic calming, the common term for the application of traffic control devices and changed road environment to a length of road, or across a local network of roads, which has the objective of reducing the speed and/or the volume of motor vehicles.** Traffic calming aims to create a road environment in which the driver and/or rider feels like the intruder in a section of road, causing them to slow down and be mindful of the needs of other road users, usually pedestrians and bicyclists. Unless a driver or rider needs to use this section of road, they may decide to seek alternate routes for future trips, thus reducing the amount of through traffic on the traffic-calmed street.

3. **Traffic-calming devices.** These may be considered in three groups:

(i) **Horizontal displacement devices.** These include chicanes,[14] refuge islands, and roundabouts, and are designed to deflect through traffic horizontally, rather than to allow it to pass through on a straight path, thus causing the driver to slow. The speed reduction achieved depends on the severity of the deflection, but in most cases reasonable drivers will pass though the chicane or roundabout at a speed of around 35–40 km/h. Note that chicanes and roundabouts must allow for service trucks (e.g., garbage trucks and removalist vans) to pass through, and therefore smaller vehicles are usually able to pass through at higher speeds. Horizontal deflection devices tend to be less effective at reducing speeds than vertical displacement devices.

(ii) **Vertical displacement devices.** These include road humps and raised intersections. They are designed to cause vehicle occupants to feel uncomfortable if their vehicle passes over the hump at a speed more than the design speed. Most road humps limit drivers to speeds of around

---

[14] A chicane changes the horizontal alignment of a road, using curb extensions, bollards, or channelization to narrow the road and create horizontal forces on the occupants of vehicles, which causes drivers to reduce speed.

Gateway signs are a positive way of introducing a regulatory speed limit as well as informing drivers and riders of changed conditions ahead. Perceptual line marking can add a positive impact to these signs (photos by Phil Jordan).

35 km/h. Because of this, road humps (flat-topped and Watts profile) have proven very effective at reducing speeds, especially in local streets. Every road hump needs to be carefully located with respect to nearby side streets and driveways, and they should not be located on steep grades. Good signage, marking, and lighting are essential features of all good road hump installations.

(iii) **Signs and line markings.** Apart from standard warning signs and regulatory speed restriction signs, a major new type of sign for a traffic-calmed area is typically placed at the entrance to each area. Commonly termed "gateway" signs, these are large signs with a conspicuous background on which there is a speed restriction (usually 30 or 40 km/h), a village or town name, and a warning about road humps ahead. A pair of gateway signs provides a conspicuous entrance into a village or town from a major road and the beginning of a package of traffic calming.

Gateway signs may be complemented by perceptual line markings along the road before and after the gateway. These markings may be a simple hatched central island, or they may be peripheral markings from the edge of the pavement at different spacings to induce a feeling of increasing speed in the driver. Most drivers then are naturally inclined to reduce speed and approach the traffic-calmed section of road in a compliant manner.

A more expensive traffic calming device is to change the road pavement so that it looks, feels, and sounds differently to the original asphalt surface. Some CAREC road authorities have replaced asphalt surfaces with cobblestones, returning the street to what it may have been like a century ago. Drivers and passengers notice the different appearance of the cobblestones on approach, can feel the change of the surface, and hear the different sound made by the tires on the cobblestones. Care should be taken when changing pavement conditions, as two-wheelers may find the new surface more slippery, and residents may complain about an increase in traffic noise.

Changing pavement surfaces is usually best considered as one part of an overall traffic-calming package. On its own, it may not achieve its speed management objectives. Modified intersection layouts—e.g., roundabouts or the closure of one or even two approaches to an intersection—are all valid options to consider when designing a traffic-calming scheme. Roundabouts are an excellent, safe form of intersection control when designed correctly. They deflect vehicles horizontally to pass through the intersection, and in this way, they reduce speeds to around 40 km/h.

A modified intersection is one in which channelization is constructed to change the priority of the junction and to modify speed in the junction. This can be an option for a national highway that makes a 90 degree turn in a small town. To facilitate the major flow of traffic, the two side streets may be truncated, narrowed, or redirected with appropriate channelization so that highway traffic proceeds with priority. But to manage speed in these situations it may be necessary to narrow the traffic lanes, lay cobblestones, or introduce another device, such as a raised intersection or a series of road humps.

Well-designed roundabouts and platform crossings in effect force speeds down and so offer consistent speed management. Speed managing treatments vary in breadth of applicability: speed limits are universally applicable, while speed humps are most suitable in urban and lower speed environments.

Roundabouts, which started as urban intersection treatments, are increasingly being adopted to manage significant intersections on higher speed roads in rural areas.

All these treatments are not only effective as retrofitted interventions for existing roads but also as design features of new roads.

Traffic calming may involve horizontal deflection devices (such as chicanes), vertical displacement devices (such as road humps), perceptual line markings, gateway signs, roundabouts, and changed surfaces, all of which aim to slow traffic and deter unnecessary traffic (photos by Phil Jordan).

Raised crossings, a vertical displacement device used to slow traffic (left photo by Eastern Alliance for Safe and Sustainable Transport and right photo by Soames Job).

A. Setting the Right Speed Limit and Operating Speed

Processes for setting speed limits vary widely across countries, including who sets the limits—the road authority or department of transport, police, or, in some countries, local authorities.

Safe speed limits are ideally determined as the road is designed. However, the selection of speed limits even for recently built roads regularly requires review, and good practice is to reassess the speed limits on 10% of a network each year, while also revising speed limits to address crash locations. Revisions are necessary because the way in which a road is used and the level of risk the road presents can change dramatically.

Safe Speed Limits

Safe speed limits are achieved by installing signs with appropriate speed limits on them, though in a few countries this may require legislative change. As the following examples demonstrate, lowering speed limits by itself lowers speeds, saving lives and avoiding injuries, including in LMICs, while preventing a substantial number of crashes and trauma.

Speed enforcement is only effective if speed limits are set at a speed low enough for safety. Effectiveness of enforcement is also reduced by high enforcement tolerances, which create higher de facto speed limits. In some countries, guaranteed enforcement tolerances of at least 10 km/h are openly interpreted by the media and community as meaning that a 40 km/h limit is really then a 50 km/h limit.

The Need to Revise Speed Limits

For road safety, it is vital to resist the mistake of setting speed limits to the "function of the road," because road function is almost always determined by vehicle traffic purposes, and thus pedestrians and cyclists are neglected. This type of process reinforces the dominance of vehicles in our thinking and is a key reason vulnerable road users are such a large proportion of crash deaths.[15] For example, it is common to find that speed limits are set to suit motor traffic with the safety needs of pedestrians for lower speeds largely ignored because traffic movement is seen as the purpose of the road. It is also common to find that roads originally intercity highways but then taken over by urban development as cities grow are still treated as highways, with high speed limits despite them in effect being urban roads, often with markets, shops, and many pedestrians. Function must be regularly reassessed based on the real use of the road, not the original intention of the road when built. Unless these changes in access and usage can be reversed, speed limits must be lowered in response to such changes.

Examples of changes to speed limits on rural and high-speed roads or motorways that were rated as "highly effective" in a World Bank review: [16]

- In Qatar, lower speed limits resulted in lower travel speeds.[17]
- In Sweden, lower speed limits on rural roads resulted in decreases in deaths and injuries, while increasing speed limits (on motorways) increased injuries.[18]
- In France, an evaluation of a reduction in the speed limit from 90 km/h to 80 km/h in many areas showed that 349 lives were saved in the first 20 months (the study was limited to 20 months to avoid any effects of the coronavirus pandemic and lockdown). The research also showed that the French population adapted to support the change relatively quickly—before the changes were introduced, 44% of men and 36% of women were strongly against it, while in June 2020 only 25% of men and 13% of women were against it.[19]

---

[15] R.F.S. Job. 2020. *Policies and Interventions to Provide Safety for Pedestrians and Overcome the Systematic Biases Underlying These Failures.* Frontiers in Sustainable Cities. 2.

[16] B. Turner, S. Job, and S. Mitra. 2021. *Guide for Road Safety Interventions: Evidence of What Works and What Does Not Work.* Washington, DC: World Bank.

[17] Author not cited. 2016. Case Study: Umm Bab Road Speed Limit Evaluation. *Qatar Road Safety Series.*

[18] A. Vadeby and Å. Forsman. 2018. *Traffic Safety Effects of New Speed Limits in Sweden.* Accident Analysis & Prevention. 114. pp. 34–39.

[19] B. McCulloch. 2020. *France's 80kph Speed Limit Saved 349 Lives – Official Report.* The Connexion. 22 July.

- In Australia, reducing a highway speed limit from 110 km/h to 100 km/h resulted in an average speed reduction and a 26.7% reduction in casualty crashes.[20]
- Belgium experienced a 33% reduction in crashes with serious injury or death when the speed limit was lowered from 90 km/h to 70 km/h.[21]
- In Australia, an initial increase in speed limit from 100 km/h to 110 km/h saw the casualty crash rate increase by around 25%, while the limit decreasing back to 100 km/h saw the casualty crash rate decrease by almost 20%.[22]
- In the United States (US), a 5 mile (8.01 km) per hour increase in the maximum state speed limit was associated with an 8% increase in fatality rates on interstate highways and freeways, and a 4% increase on other roads. An estimated 33,000 more people were killed in crashes during 1995–2013 than would have occurred if maximum speed limits had not increased.[23]

CAREC and Other examples:

- Increasing speed limits from 70 km/h to 80 km/h in Hong Kong, China increased fatal crashes by 36% and fatal and serious injury crashes by 18%.[24]

Examples on urban and low-speed roads:

- Mass reductions in the speed limit from 30 to 25 miles per hour in New York City led to substantial reductions in crashes and injuries.[25]
- Speed limit reductions in Auckland, New Zealand's largest city, resulted in a 67% reduction in fatalities and a 20% reduction in all injury crashes.[26]
- Urban speed limit reductions from 60 km/h to 50 km/h in Australia resulted in mean speeds reduced by 3.8 km/h, yielding a 23% reduction in casualty (fatal and injury) crashes. In addition, the effect of lowering speeds did not dissipate, but was stronger after 3 years than 1 year, demonstrating that the benefits sustain well, and people get used to the new limits.[27]
- Savings of crash trauma through speed limit reductions are also in evidence in Canada,[28] and elsewhere.[29]

CAREC and Other examples:

- Increasing speed limits from 50 km/h to 70 km/h in Hong Kong, China resulted in a 15% increase in fatal and serious injury crashes (footnote 23).
- Increasing speed limits on arterial roads in Ankara, Türkiye, led to an increase in crashes.[30]
- A program of lowering speed limits in Brazil resulted in 1,889 fewer crashes within the first 18 months of the change, reducing crashes by 21.7% on roads with lower limits, with larger effects on roads with camera-based enforcement.[31]

---

[20] Y. Bhatnagar et al. 2010. *Changes to Speed Limits and Crash Outcome: Great Western Highway Case Study.* In Proceedings of the Australasian Road Safety Research, Policing and Education Conference. 14.

[21] E. De Pauw et al. 2014. Safety Effects of Reducing the Speed Limit from 90 km/h to 70 km/h. *Accident Analysis & Prevention.* 62. pp. 426–431.

[22] J. Sliogeris. 1992. *One Hundred and Ten Kilometre per Hour Speed Limit: Evaluation of Road Safety Effects.* Carlton, Australia: VIC Roads.

[23] C.M. Farmer. 2017. Relationship of Traffic Fatality Rates to Maximum State Speed Limits. *Traffic Injury Prevention.* 18 (4). pp. 375–380.

[24] S.C. Wong et al. 2005. Would Relaxing Speed Limits Aggravate Safety? A Case Study of Hong Kong. *Accident Analysis & Prevention.* 37 (2). pp. 377–388.

[25] K. Mammen, H. S. Shim, and B.S. Weber. 2020. Vision Zero: Speed Limit Reduction and Traffic Injury Prevention in New York City. *Eastern Economic Journal.* 46 (2). pp. 282–300.

[26] Auckland Transport. 2021. Safe Speeds Update. 24 September.

[27] C.N. Kloeden, J.E. Woolley, and A. McLean. 2007. *A Follow-Up Evaluation of the 50km/h Default Urban Speed Limit in South Australia.* Road Safety Research, Education and Policing Conference in Melbourne, Australia, 17–19 October 2007.

[28] M.T. Isla and K. El-Basyouny. 2015. Full Bayesian Evaluation of the Safety Effects of Reducing the Posted Speed Limit in Urban Residential Area. *Accident Analysis & Prevention.* 80. pp. 18–25.

[29] K. Neki et al. 2021. Economic Impact of 30km/h—Benefits and Costs of Speeds in an Urban Environment. *Journal of Road Safety.* 32 (3). pp. 49–51.

[30] F. Ture Kiba and H. Tuydes-Yaman. 2020. GIS-Based Evaluation of the Speed Limit Increase on Urban Arterial Traffic Safety in Ankara. *Arabian Journal of Geosciences.* 13 (12). pp. 1–16.

[31] A. Ang, P. Christensen, and R. Vieira. 2020. Should Congested Cities Reduce Their Speed Limits? Evidence from São Paulo, Brazil. *Journal of Public Economics.* 184. 104155.

- Other examples include savings of crash trauma through speed limit reductions in Ukraine [32] and the potential savings for lower speed limits in Thailand.[33]

School Zone and Pedestrian Area Speed Limits

The safe system speed limit for pedestrians is 30 km/h. This includes school children, though due to additional risks—including their lower height meaning reduced visibility and capacity to survive a crash—lower than this is ideal for school zones. The 30 km/h speed limits are common in good-performing road safety countries such as the Netherlands, Norway, Sweden, and Switzerland, with 20 km/h also increasingly in use for pedestrian and residential areas (see Figure 1 for examples). A 30 km/h speed limit is best introduced along with traffic calming interventions.

Georgia has adopted 30 km/h limits in many school zones in Tbilisi, Zugdidi, and Rustavi, and in various instances included engineering measures to reduce speeds.[34] The People's Republic of China (PRC) has 30 km/h speed limits on many urban roads with single lanes in each direction (Box 1). Other CAREC countries have also introduced 30 km/h zones but significant expansions of their use would be valuable.

Speed limit-setting practices in CAREC countries are improving, but need to go further. For example, in Mongolia, speed limits are set by road engineers for new roads, and can be revised if a crash black-spot is identified or through road safety audits, which are gradually increasing in use. In 2018, the rules on speed limit setting were amended to allow for consideration of crash risk. These are sound practices, which could nonetheless still be improved through greater focus on providing speeds that protect vulnerable road users, the setting of lower default speed limits including where pedestrians are present, and further expanded use of well-trained auditors explicitly directed to consider speed limits.

Box 1: Business and Economic Benefits of a 30-Kilometer Per Hour Zone in Shanghai

In the early 2000s, Yangpu District in Shanghai, People's Republic of China was developed into an urban office, retail, and mixed-use community known as a Knowledge and Innovation Community (KIC), replacing its previous residential and industrial functions. Daxue Road, the main road in the KIC, was renovated in 2012. Major improvements included setting the speed limit to 30 kilometers per hour, enforced with speed cameras, to facilitate safe pedestrian activity and quieter streets; refurbishing sidewalks to encourage restaurants to open outdoor seating and revitalize street activities; using corners with a small turning radius of 5 meters to physically slow vehicle speeds; and installing planters and bike parking racks. During the planning phase, block sizes were reduced, creating more signalized intersections and reducing the opportunity for excessive vehicle speeds in mid-blocks. Surrounding streets were also changed to make the wider KIC area walking- and biking-friendly. For example, sidewalk curbs were extended to narrow the street, pocket parks were constructed, and flower boxes were used to block excessive parking spaces.

Through such improvements, the area has attracted over 400 small businesses and 200 start-ups. Rents in the KIC rose 30% higher than in other business areas in Yangpu District, and are among the highest in Shanghai. This road is now a well-recognized example of urban revitalization in the People's Republic of China.

Sources: A. B. Sharpin et al. 2021. Low Speed Zone Guide. Washington, DC: World Resources Institute & Global Road Safety Facility; Qian, Chen. 2017. Daxuelu shinian yanbian dui jiedao fuxing de qishi (Implication of the 10-Year Daxue Road Evolution on Street Revival). Shidai jianzhu 6, (11). pp. Sept. 2017): 55–61; and Xu, Miao, and Kaiyun Zhang. Chuangke tiandi (Innospace) Shanghai: Urban Land Institute Case Study. 2015.

---

[32] A. Ryabushenko et al. 2021. Effect of Speed Limit Reduction from 60 to 50 km/h on Road Safety for a Large Ukrainian City. In AIP Conference Proceedings. 2439 (1). p. 020021.

[33] World Bank. 2019. *Speed Variation Analysis: A Case Study for Thailand's Roads*. Washington, DC.

[34] Global Alliance of NGOs for Road Safety. 2023. 96 School Zones Adopt 30 km/h Speed Limit in 3 Municipalities in Georgia. *Global Alliance of NGOs for Road Safety Newsletter*. 27 January.

A pilot project that reduces speed limits to 30 kilometers per hour (km/h) in Bishkek, Kyrgyz Republic (photo by EASST).

Road with a 30 km/h speed limit in Azerbaijan (photo by Soames Job).

Road with a 30 km/h speed limit in Georgia combined with a speed hump (photo by Soames Job).

A road with a 20 km/h speed limit, increasingly in use in Europe combined with traffic calming (photo by Soames Job).

The World Bank rated 30 km/h zones for pedestrians as "highly effective" (footnote 17). Some practical examples of these zones being implemented include:

- Austria's Graz, which in 1992 became the first city in Europe to introduce a 30 km/h speed limit. This now applies to almost 80% of the city's road network, including all residential roads, school zones, and areas near hospitals. The scheme's objectives were to increase safety and reduce pollution and noise. On roads where a 30 km/h speed limit has been implemented, the number of crashes has decreased by 25%, and over 80% of all crashes in the city take place on through roads where the speed limit is still 50 km/h.
- In Switzerland, 30 km/h limits reduced crashes by 38%.[35]
- In Canada's Toronto, speed limit reductions from 40 to 30 km/h resulted in a 28% reduction in pedestrian crashes between 2013 and 2018 and a 67% reduction in serious and fatal injuries on streets after the 30 km/h limit had been implemented (along with signage and some red-light cameras)—more than twice the reductions achieved on control streets.[36]

---

[35] European Transport Safety Council (ETSC). 2023. Swiss Research Shows 30 km/h Zones Reduced Crashes by 38%. 21 March.

[36] L. Fridman. 2020. Effect of Reducing the Posted Speed Limit to 30 km per hour on Pedestrian Motor Vehicle Collisions in Toronto, Canada – A Quasi Experimental, Pre-Post Study. BMC Public Health. 20 (1). pp. 1–8.

- Reducing speed limits around schools to 40 km/h in the Australian state of New South Wales (NSW) delivered pedestrian casualty crash reductions of 45% and an all-crash reduction of 35%.[37] Australia is now increasing the number of 30 km/h zones.
- In Qatar, raised platforms were among the treatments adopted to successfully and substantially reduce vehicle speeds at school zones.[38]

Another aspect of special speed limits relates to weather conditions. For example, some countries have lower speed limits on various roads when it is raining. In CAREC countries, this may be best adopted for when there is snow, which adds to risk. For example, Kazakhstan data from KazAutoZhol, which manages national highways, reveal that the peak months for crash deaths are November, December, and August. The latter reflects holiday travel, while the winter peak is likely to be weather-related and occurs despite reduced travel in winter.

Motorway in Kazakhstan with median barriers, yet with elevated risk of serious crash due to snow (photo by Soames Job).

Improved Speed Limit Signage, with No Change of Limit

While many countries have improved their signage, including installing reminders of the speed limit, these programs are rarely evaluated. Suitable evaluations that include any crash data are rare. In Australia however, it was shown that speed limits are most effective when prominently displayed and thus known to drivers. For example, simply adding more 60 km/h speed limit signs to remind drivers of the limit (with no change in speed limit) reduced speeds by 2.1 km/h on roads where the limit signs were erected. This resulted in a 16% reduction in casualty crashes.

B. Prioritizing Road Design and Engineering Opportunities

With one exception, all examples of speed managing infrastructure, or traffic calming, are more forceful in reducing speeds than simply advising the driver to reduce speed. Thus, these are to be preferred for their direct role without reliance on a compliant driver. Safe speed limits are the exception, relying on the drivers choosing to comply with the limit. However, the evidence for strong road safety gains from lower speed limits proves that drivers are influenced by lower speed limits. Gateway treatments may in some instances act as more visible speed limits, unless traffic calming features such as road narrowing or raised platforms are included.

Another opportunity for maintaining higher speeds with safety exists in transforming open-access motorways or arterial roads into managed motorways with access controls (i.e., no pedestrian access, access for vehicles restricted to locations with merge and/or acceleration lanes, and exits restricted to locations where deceleration lanes can be provided). This has major advantages in terms of affording significantly more safety, as well as allowing for smoother traffic flow at higher speeds than with open access maintained, generating less fuel use and fewer emissions. In some locations, the process of changing speed limits must be coordinated with other operational processes, such as traffic operations and signal phasing. In addition, a lower speed limit may influence road features and design, such as horizonal and vertical alignment.

---

[37] A. Graham and P. Sparkes. 2010. Casualty Reductions in NSW Associated with the 40 km/h School Zone Initiative. *2010 Australasian Road Safety, Research, Policing and Education Conference*. 31 August–3 September 2010. Canberra.

[38] F. Marsh. M. De Roos, and R. Webster. 2016. Peer Review Papers. *Journal of the Australasian College of Road Safety*. 27 (3).

C. Recommendations for Road Design and Engineering

The following recommendations may be considered:

- Traffic calming infrastructure delivers significant road safety benefits and is recommended for widespread adoption in CAREC countries and elsewhere. The most powerful examples include vertical deflection (speed humps, speed cushions, raised intersections, raised crossings, and raised platforms) and horizontal deflection (roundabouts, chicanes). Research shows that in lower speed-zoned areas, engineering measures, such as speed humps and speed cushions, are more effective than enforcement. Vertical deflection treatments delivery twice the reduction in injury crashes achieved by speed cameras. Traffic calming should be visible to drivers via signage warnings and/or by visible painting of the traffic calming device.
- It is important to use the many studies provided to dismiss the view that traffic calming measures, such as speed humps, lead to an increase in crashes. Crashes occasionally happen anywhere and when they occur around speed humps, drivers and motorcycle riders tend to blame the speed hump. Speed humps however lead to impressive reductions in serious crashes.
- Many CAREC countries use speed humps but these are not common in many locations where they would be a suitable solution for speeding. Changes to standards and guidelines are recommended to specify the many circumstances where speed humps should be required or at least recommended, rather than allowed.
- Highly visible gateway treatments with traffic calming measures such as a raised platform, speed hump, and/or lane narrowing are effective and should be adopted at the entry to urban or village areas where the speed limit changes.
- Area-wide use of traffic calming is especially cost-effective and recommended.
- Lane narrowing is a less definitive measure, but has nonetheless been proven to reduce serious crash numbers, and so is also recommended. This should not be achieved by reducing the width of the road, which can be harmful to safety, but by painting lane lines to reduce lane width and increase road shoulder width, and/or by changing median lines to create wide center lines with profile line-marking (rumble strips). Wide center lines are a proven road safety treatment.[39]
- Lower speed limits, especially set to safe system speeds, save lives and injuries and are also recommended, along with increased speed limit signage and gateway treatments. These should ideally be combined with traffic calming and enforcement for improved speed limit compliance.
- The effectiveness of enforcement is best maintained by avoiding high enforcement tolerances, which create higher de facto speed limits.
- For school zones and areas with significant pedestrian movements, speeds should be 30 km/h or lower, and should be managed with traffic calming interventions as well as speed limits of 30 km/h or lower.
- Road safety speed limits and the ideal speed of traffic should not be set based on the function of the road because the function is almost always determined based on vehicle traffic purposes, and thus pedestrians and cyclists are seriously neglected. This type of process reinforces the dominance of vehicles and is a key part of the cause of vulnerable road users being such a large proportion of crash deaths (footnote 15). Instead, either the supposed function should be ignored or the assessment of function must be refined to include pedestrians and cycle users as well as surrounding land use. The function should also be regularly reassessed based on the real use of the road, not the original intention of the road when built.
- Speed limit-setting practices in CAREC countries can be improved through revision of default speed limits to safe system levels, with increased consideration of vulnerable road users, rather than a focus on the road itself in setting default and actual speed limits.
- Greater use of well-trained auditors, who assess travel speeds and consider the lowering of speeds as a method for reducing risk, is also recommended.

---

[39] D. J. Connell et al. 2010. *Trial Evaluation of Wide Tactile Center Line Configurations on the Newell Highway*. In Proceedings of the 2010 Australasian Road Safety Research, Policing and Education Conference. Canberra. September.

III. Vehicle Technology

Vehicle technologies offer important opportunities to help manage travel speeds albeit with implementation challenges. These are considered in this module.

A. Challenges of Improving Vehicle Technology

Vehicle technologies can substantially improve the management of speed and thus save many lives and debilitating injuries. While they have existed for years, vehicle manufacturers have only adopted them minimally for cars and heavy vehicles. A key reason for the lack of adoption is the common view that high speed is fun and safe, so drivers do not want their vehicle to stop them from speeding and will be reluctant to buy a vehicle that limits speeds to the legal limits. The argument that market forces will create demand for speed managing technologies is therefore mistaken in current cultural circumstances; nevertheless, it is promoted to avoid government regulation requiring these technologies. Indeed, government regulation requiring speed managing technologies is slow, rare, and even when it does occur the regulations, though valuable, require less than ideal versions of the available technologies.

Assessing Road Safety Value

Evaluations of the road safety benefits of vehicles are complex, and thus few can be cited. The main source of complexity is that vehicle technology comes into a vehicle fleet gradually and so a clear start to any change in crashes cannot be identified. Even when a technology is mandated, that technology has always existed in many vehicles before regulation is adopted. Thus, the evidence for the value of vehicle technology arises from assessments of the effects of the technology in experiments combined with estimates of the number of crashes that this technology will address. As a hypothetical example, the value of the introduction of electronic stability control (ESC), a technology to reduce loss of control crashes, can be estimated as follows: One third of all single vehicle fatal crashes in the US involve a rollover, so if ESC can avoid 20% of these crashes (estimated from experiments with the technology), then adding ESC to all vehicles in the US would eliminate 6.6% (20% of 33%) of single vehicle fatal crashes.[40]

For this reason, evaluations from various countries are generally limited. As this is direct technology, it can be expected to work the same way across countries, but safety benefits achieved may vary and each country will need to assess their relevant crash data to estimate their likely value. For example, in the above case of ESC, lives saved will depend on how many fatal crashes involve run-off-road and rollover crashes for a particular country.

B. Vehicle Interventions to Help Limit Speed

Technological interventions can be used to help limit speeds, and include the following:

(i) **Advisory intelligent speed adaptation and speed-governing advisory intelligent speed adaptation.** Intelligent speed adaptation or assistance (ISA) involves advanced vehicle technology systems to determine the speed limits applicable for the vehicle in its current location. These assist or force drivers to stick to the speed limit. These technologies use a global navigation satellite system, such as a global positioning system (GPS) linked to a speed zone database and thus allows the vehicle (or the mobile phone) to "know" its location and the speed limit on that road.

---

[40] E.K. Liebemann et al. 2004. Safety and Performance Enhancement: The Bosch Electronic Stability Control (ESC). *SAE Paper.* 20004. pp. 21–0060.

The actions of the vehicle in response to the speed information can vary. Advisory ISA systems provide visual (and usually auditory) feedback to the driver if the vehicle exceeds the speed limit. Some versions of advisory ISA systems beep to the driver when the speed limit is exceeded, and others provide stronger cues such as a beep and reverse pressure on the accelerator pedal which requires the driver to deliberately push harder to exceed the limit. Speed-governing or intervening ISA limits the speed of the vehicle to the speed limit, with the driver having to take action to slow down, though typically the threshold for the intervention can be changed or the system can be turned off.

These systems have been trialed in many countries. A review of evidence shows that available ISA technologies currently represent an efficient and effective way of controlling speeding and thus improving road safety immediately. These systems are relatively cheap and easy to fit in new vehicles and to retrofit to existing vehicles.[41] In Sweden and the Netherlands, trials highlight that driver acceptability is an issue,[42] ISA systems that the driver can readily override produce weak results with large variations among drivers,[43] and the systems tend to be overridden by drivers when ISA is most needed.[44] In the United Kingdom (UK), ISA systems that intervene produce powerful road safety gains. Carsten and Tate assessed that an intervening ISA system is "the most powerful collision avoidance system currently available." They subsequently estimated that in the UK, ISA that prevents vehicles exceeding the speed limit would save 20% of injury crashes and 37% of fatal crashes. A more complex version of the mandatory system, including a capability to limit speeds to current network and weather conditions, would result in a reduction of 36% in injury crashes and 59% in fatal crashes. Benefit–cost ratios (BCRs) for this implementation strategy were in a range of 7.9–15.4, reflecting savings impressively larger than the costs of the scheme.[45]

Meanwhile in the PRC, a simulation study evaluating the effects of ISA found that because fuel consumption and emissions are related to acceleration, deceleration, and speed, fuel consumption would decrease by about 8% if all vehicles adopted ISA, thereby reducing emissions.[46]

An effective speed-reducing technology only delivers strong road safety benefits if the technology is introduced to new or imported vehicles so that over time the whole fleet has the technology. Genuinely effective speed-reducing technology will not be adopted into all vehicles through market forces, because some drivers want to speed freely and not be limited in doing so by their vehicle. These drivers are also the reason that partial implementation does not deliver significant benefits—because the drivers who need the technology the most are those who avoid adopting it or are most likely to override it (Box 2).

(ii) **Vehicle speed limiters speed governing.** Vehicle speed limiters involve technology installed in a vehicle that prevents the motor from moving the vehicle beyond a single set speed. This differs from ISA by having only one limit rather than being sensitive to the prevailing speed limit. Thus, it is normally applied for the highest safe speed for the vehicle. For example, in Australia's NSW, heavy vehicles (trucks and buses) are limited to 100 km/h by technology in the vehicle, even if the speed limits for the road is 110 km/h, such as on some motorways.[47] Heavy penalties apply for attempts to interfere with the speed-limiting technology. Effective enforcement has been challenging, though

---

[41] M. Ryan. 2019. *Intelligent Speed Assistance Technologies: A Review.* In Proceedings of the Irish Transport Research Network (IRTN) Conference.

[42] T. Biding and G. Lind. 2002. *Intelligent Speed Adaptation (ISA): Results of Large-Scale Trials in Borlange, Lidkoping, Lund and Umea During 1999–2002.* No. 2002: 89 E.

[43] S. Vlassenroot et al. 2007. Driving with Intelligent Speed Adaptation: Final Results of the Belgian ISA-trial. *Transportation Research Part A: Policy and Practice.* 41 (3). pp. 267–279.

[44] F. Lai and O. Carsten. 2012. What Benefit Does Intelligent Speed Adaptation Deliver: A Close Examination of its Effect on Vehicle Speeds. *Accident Analysis & Prevention.* 48. pp. 4–9.

[45] O. M. Carsten and F. N. Tate. 2005. Intelligent Speed Adaptation: Accident Savings and Cost–Benefit Analysis. *Accident Analysis & Prevention.* 37 (3). pp. 407–416.

[46] J. Li et al. 2009. *Intelligent Speed Adaptation Impact of Fuel Consumption and Emission.* Paper prepared for International Conference on Transportation Engineering 2009. pp. 1311–1316.

[47] NSW Government. 2019. Speed Limiter Compliance Fact Sheet for the Heavy Vehicle Industry. December.

Box 2: The Introduction of Regulations for Speed Managing Technology in the European Union

The European Commission (EC) approved Regulation (EU) 2021/1958 on 23 June 2021, requiring a suite of vehicle safety technologies, including intelligent speed assistance (ISA) in new models in the European Union (EU), for all vehicles in production from 6 July 2024. This is the first such regulated requirement for ISA anywhere in the world. Importantly, it highlights that such regulations are feasible for many countries and regions, and will eventually provide a significant step forward for the safety of secondhand vehicles being exported to low- and middle-income countries from the EU.

The required ISA system prompts and encourages drivers to slow down when they are over the speed limit. The system works with the driver as an assisting function, through the accelerator control, or through other dedicated, appropriate, and effective feedback, while the driver remains in full control of the driving speed of the vehicle. It is an effective safety measure because even a slightly reduced driving speed has a significant beneficial effect on crash avoidance or mitigation of crash severity. The EU regulation will initially allow manufacturers to choose between four technical options as follows:

(1) a haptic feedback system that relies on the pedal restoring force—where the driver's foot is gently pushed back in case of over-speed—which will help to reduce driving speed and can be overridden by the driver;
(2) the speed control system, which relies on engine management, and involves an automatic reduction of the propulsion power independent of the position of the driver's foot on the pedal, but can also be overridden by the driver easily;
(3) a cascaded acoustic warning, with an initial flash as an optical signal and then, after several seconds, if no reaction is detected, an acoustic warning is activated, then if the driver ignores this combined feedback, both warnings are timed out; and
(4) a cascaded vibration warning, where the first step is an optical flash, then after several seconds, if no reaction is detected, the pedal vibrates, then if the driver ignores this combined feedback, both warnings are timed out.

There was substantial resistance and pressure from vehicle manufacturers to remove ISA systems from the proposed regulations and replace them with just a speed limit display, which is not supported by research evidence on best practice. This pushback was resisted by many road safety experts, including the Towards Zero Foundation and the European Transport Safety Council. The inclusion by the EC of the cascading warning options represented a compromise position that was included in the final regulation. By December 2025, the EC will review the ISA options included in the regulation and consider a possible amendment to remove the option for cascading warning systems, which evidence suggests are less effective.

Source: J. Li et al. 2009. *Intelligent Speed Adaptation Impact of Fuel Consumption and Emission*. Paper prepared for International Conference on Transportation Engineering 2009. pp. 1311–1316.

improving. In Canada, in a survey of truck operators, most reported that their speed limiters were improving safety and creating other benefits such as reducing tire wear.[48] In Europe, a simulation study found that speed limiters added to light goods vehicles would generate strong safety benefits, and achieve a strong BCR of 2.5–4.5 (i.e., for each dollar spend there is a return of $2.50–$4.50 in savings).[49] In the US meanwhile, a comparison of trucks with and without speed limiters showed that those without limiters have 200% more speed limiter-relevant crashes.[50]

---

[48] R. Bishop. 2008. Safety Impacts of Speed Limiter Device Installations on Commercial Trucks and Buses. Vol. 16. Transportation Research Board.

[49] T. Toledo, G. Albert, and S. Hakkert. 2007. Impact of Active Speed Limiters on Traffic Flow and Safety: Simulation-Evaluation. *Transportation Research Record*. 2019 (1). pp. 169–180.

[50] J.S. Hickman et al. 2012. Safety Benefits of Speed Limiters in Commercial Motor Vehicles Using Carrier-Collected Crash Data. *Journal of Intelligent Transportation Systems*. 16 (4). pp. 177–183.

(iii) **Speed monitoring.** The speed of a vehicle can be continuously monitored via GPS data or by a tachograph fitted to the vehicle. A tachograph or tachometer provides a record of engine speed over an extended period. These are mainly used in commercial road vehicles.

There are two common forms of use of continuous speed monitoring. First, private transport companies may continuously monitor the speeds of their vehicles, especially trucks. As an example, in Europe tachographs are mandatory for all new heavy goods vehicles and for buses carrying more than nine people. Since June 2019, a new generation of tachographs are being installed in newly registered trucks and buses. These smart tachographs include enhanced anti-tampering, additional communication tools such as vehicle location positioning, and transmission of real-time information to enforcement authorities by means of a short-range communication channel. This enhances enforcement of speed limits by these vehicles. However, the enforcement has not focused on speeding, which could be added to the current focus on driving hours and rest periods. Thus, no relevant evaluation exists.

Many trucking and logistics companies continuously monitor the speeds of their vehicles (possibly in addition to other driving features) with data fed directly back to monitoring centers run by these companies. The efficacy of such systems is likely to depend on the policies adopted regarding the consequences for the speeding driver, and while trials have been reported as underway, evaluations are scarce.[51]

C. Prioritizing Vehicle Technology Opportunities

Based on available evaluations, the high priority opportunity vehicle technology for improved speed management is clearly intervening ISA that cannot be overridden by the driver. Advisory ISA is second priority, though the benefits are significantly weaker.

Some apparently promising vehicle technologies to manage speed have been in use for many years, yet rigorous evaluations of safety benefits are absent. With delivery of such evaluations, priorities in this area may change.

D. Recommendations for Vehicle Technology

The following recommendations may be considered:

- Mandatory intervening ISA that cannot be overridden by the driver are recommended as the strongest vehicle technology opportunity for speed management. This can be regulated for all new and imported vehicles with a reasonable start date.
- Speed limiters that limit vehicles (especially trucks, buses, and goods vans) to a maximum speed equal to or lower than the speed limit on rural roads (not highways) are recommended, with studies indicating clear safety and other benefits.
- Vehicle industry advice on the start date was proven to be false in the European Union (EU) regulation of ISA systems, and so in future should be interpreted with concern for self-interest.
- Mandating installation of advisory ISA systems is recommended as a weaker opportunity, but still worthwhile.
- Rigorous evaluations of vehicle technologies such as speed monitoring are needed before evidence-based recommendations on these can be made.

---

[51] N. Haworth, C. Tingvall, and N. Kowadlo. 2000. Review of Best Practice Road Safety Initiatives in the Corporate and/or Business Environment. *Monash University Accident Research Centre Reports.* 166, 119.

IV. Changing Road-User Behavior

The behavior of road users is often seen as the cause of crash deaths and injuries.[52] Various studies and reports of crash data have been cited to show that most crashes involve road user error. However, the problems with this approach are increasingly recognized, notably including that such studies do not consider the extent to which other elements of the system could have avoided the serious crash (footnote 15). For example, even with human error, head-on crashes can be avoided through median crash barriers. Nonetheless, no country has yet achieved a road system that delivers a safe system and thus saves everyone from errors. For this reason, changing road user behavior remains a potent way to improve road safety, as many examples cited in this module demonstrate. Even in HICs, such as those in Europe, improving behavior is powerful; the European Transport Safety Council has estimated that enforcing all laws could decrease crash deaths in the EU by 50%.[53]

This module describes the deeper psychological reasons for certain approaches to instigate road user behavior change being more effective than others. It presents the most effective actions to take to instigate change, identifies some ineffective actions, and provides the evidence for these ratings of effectiveness.

A. Enforcement and Communications

There is no doubt that well-delivered enforcement works, especially when supported with the right communications and campaigns. The evidence reveals a clear relationship between enforcement and crashes, with more enforcement leading to reductions in crashes (Figure 1). There are also ways to increase the effectiveness of a set amount of enforcement, provided in the following sections.

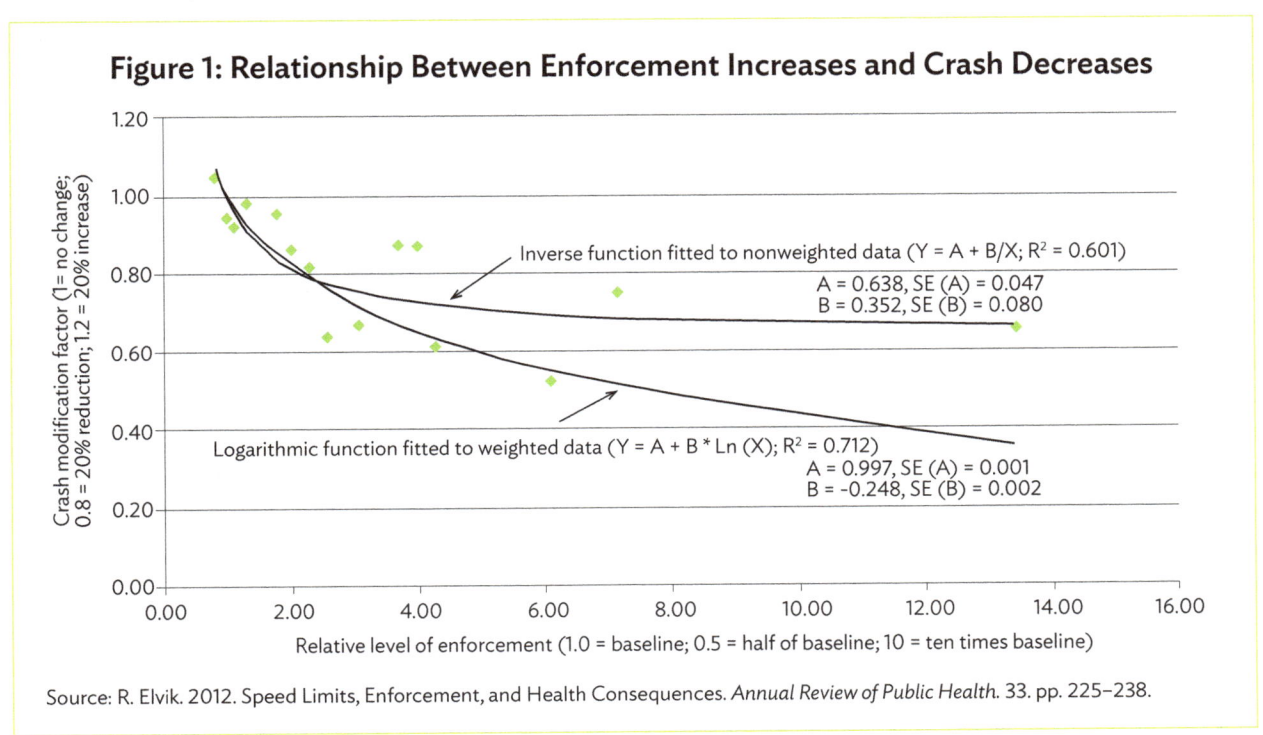

Figure 1: Relationship Between Enforcement Increases and Crash Decreases

Inverse function fitted to nonweighted data (Y = A + B/X; R^2 = 0.601)
A = 0.638, SE (A) = 0.047
B = 0.352, SE (B) = 0.080

Logarithmic function fitted to weighted data (Y = A + B * Ln (X); R^2 = 0.712)
A = 0.997, SE (A) = 0.001
B = -0.248, SE (B) = 0.002

Source: R. Elvik. 2012. Speed Limits, Enforcement, and Health Consequences. *Annual Review of Public Health*. 33. pp. 225–238.

---

[52] E.g., Alice in Blunderland (1947) - YouTube
[53] ETSC. 1999. *Police Enforcement Strategies to Reduce Traffic Casualties in Europe*. Brussels.

Challenges Faced by Low- and Middle-Income Countries in Instigating Behavior Change

LMICs face many challenges in delivering effective enforcement and campaigns, despite police often contributing significantly to government revenue through fines.[54] These challenges include:

- lack of sufficient funding for campaigns;
- poor media channels to reach the audience with campaigns and messages;
- lack of enforcement equipment (e.g., speed guns);
- lack of patrol vehicles and funding for fuel;
- speed limit signage too infrequent and vandalized or stolen, for scrap metal or other purposes;[55]
- use of road police for traffic management rather than safety-related enforcement;
- poor data management preventing license loss and other penalties being effectively applied;
- lack of effective enforcement at night;
- the absence of effective follow-up mechanisms to ensure timely payment of fines;
- police fear of wealthy or powerful drivers who are thus able to break the law with impunity;
- weak judicial systems that allow offenders to avoid penalties; and
- public perceptions that the penalty can be avoided.[56]

With stronger business cases for road safety to improve funding, careful use of resources, and rigorously evidence-based approaches (such as shifting from an education-based approach to a publicized enforcement approach), strong road safety improvements are still possible.

How to Achieve Behavior Change: The Aim of Enforcement and Communications

Evidence shows that often the best way to change behavior is a direct approach to the behavior, which will result in a later change in attitudes to match the behavior. Psychology, and indeed road safety, are filled with examples where a change of attitude or belief does not result in the expected change in behavior, but of examples where forcing a change in behavior, such as through strong enforcement, results in a change in attitude.[57]

Almost always, the true aim of road safety enforcement and communications must be behavior change. The communications and advertising industry have long promoted the view that their aim is attitude and belief change; this suits the industry because it is easy, fast, and relatively cheap to show that these happened. However, too often people will report that a particular message has changed their view of speeding, but they will continue to speed as before. No crashes will be avoided through changes in attitude and belief unless the right behavior change follows, and often it does not.

Occasionally, a communications campaign may be needed to explain the need for enforcement, typically to a vocal minority who oppose the enforcement, so that the political will for enforcement is enhanced.[58] Such a campaign should not be expected to improve road user behavior as well, but only to change attitudes and verbal expressions of them. Thus, employing such a campaign is appropriate in cases where there is a reasonable chance of a decision to implement a strong intervention (such as speed cameras or other improvements to speeding deterrence) and where the necessary political will is not yet sufficient, but may reasonably be achieved after such a campaign.

---

[54] See, for instance, Annual Traffic and Road Safety Report. 2016. Road Safety Performance Review: Uganda equipment.

[55] United Nations Economic Commission for Africa & United Nations Economic Commission for Europe. 2018. *Road Safety Performance Review Uganda*. New York and Geneva.

[56] This list is based on the author's direct experiences in many countries including road safety management capacity reviews, and United Nations Economic Commission for Africa & United Nations Economic Commission for Europe. 2018. *Road Safety Performance Review Uganda*. New York and Geneva.

[57] R.F.S. Job, T. Prabhakar, and S.H.V. Lee. 1997. *The Long-Term Benefits of Random Breath Testing in NSW (Australia): Deterrence and Social Disapproval of Drink-Driving*. In C. Mercier-Guyon (ed). 1997. Proceedings of the 14th International Conference on Alcohol, Drugs and Traffic Safety. pp. 841–848. France: CERMT; and R.F.S. Job. 1988. Effective and Ineffective Use of Fear in Health Promotion Campaigns. *American Journal of Public Health*. 78. pp. 163–167.

[58] For example, in the UK, there is broad support for speed cameras, but a vocal minority opposition. See H. Wells. 2012. *The Fast and the Furious: Drivers, Speed Cameras and Control in a Risk Society*. Surrey, England & Burlington, US: Ashgate Publishing.

The Psychological Nature of Road Safety: A Motivation Problem

In road-user behavior, road safety is largely a motivation problem.[59] Most instances of speeding are deliberate, which is to say these behaviors are chosen by the relevant road users, not forced upon them, or inadvertent. This means that these behaviors were motivated. Against this view, drivers will often claim that they did not know the speed limit, or did not notice that they were speeding. However, evidence indicates otherwise, with drivers commonly slowing down for speed cameras and speeding up after they are past the camera.[60] The following points are key:

- *Speeding is not a knowledge problem.* Most drivers know what a speed limit sign means, but many choose to ignore it.
- *Speeding is not a skill problem.* It does not take more skill to drive at or under 60 km/h in a 60 km/h zone than to drive at 70 km/h in a 60 km/h zone.
- *Speeding is a motivation problem.* Drivers are motivated to drive faster and are likely to do so without effective deterrence to sufficiently motivate them to obey the speed limit.
- *Crash risk does not stop speeding.* For psychological reasons, the risk of even a serious crash does not provide a general motivation to stay within the speed limit, whereas enforcement can provide this motivation.

Realizing that road safety is a motivation issue explains why these behaviors persist, and several key road safety traps can then be avoided by understanding the following:

- Enforcement provides a motivation to not speed due to the risk of being caught and punished.
- Education provides knowledge. However, speeding is not a knowledge problem, so education is not likely to help road safety beyond the very basics (red means stop, what a speed limit sign means, etc).
- Driving skills are not critical to the main contributors to death and suffering from crashes. Wearing a safety-belt or a helmet or choosing not to drive after drinking alcohol are motivated choices, not skill problems. These behaviors require strong motivation to comply. Thus, driver skills training is not helpful, and can even cause an increase in crashes in those who are trained;[61] the same pattern occurs for motorcycle rider skills training.[62] The evidence shows that increasing driver skills increases driver overconfidence, which increases risk-taking ("I have more skill, so I can take a risk");[63] however, there is good news for some forms of driver training: many hours of on-road supervised practice, not deliberate skills training, reduces crash rates for novice drivers.[64]

Positive Emotions and the Perceived Value of Behaviors That Reduce Road Safety

For many reasons, including deliberate misinformation promulgated from various sources, and positive promotion of speed from various parts of the private sector (Appendix 1), community as well as political and decision-maker views of some risky on-road behaviors remain positive, especially speeding (Module VII). Risk-taking, including speeding in particular, has a strong positive value for young drivers,[65] who are at greatest risk of speeding crashes.[66]

---

[59] R. F. S. Job. 1999. The Psychology of Driving and Road Safety. In J. Clark, ed. *Current Issues in Road Safety Research and Practice.* pp. 21–55. Armidale, Australia: EMU Press.

[60] R. F. S. Job. 2013. *Pillar 1 Road Safety Management–Speed management.* Paper prepared for the Transportation Research Board Annual Meeting, TRB Sunday Workshop: Pivotal Role of Speed Management across the Five Road Safety Pillars. Washington, DC. January.

[61] B. Jones. 1995. The Effectiveness of Skid-Car Training for Teenage Novice Drivers in Oregon. *The Chronicle of American Driver & Traffic Safety Education Association.* 43 (1). pp. 1–8.

[62] R. Q. Ivers et al. 2016. Does an On-Road Motorcycle Coaching Program Reduce Crashes in Novice Riders? A Randomised Control Trial. *Accident Analysis & Prevention.* 86. pp. 40–46.

[63] A. Katila et al. 2004. Does Increased Confidence Among Novice Drivers Imply a Decrease in Safety? The Effects of Skid Training on Slippery Road Accidents. *Accident Analysis & Prevention.* 36 (4), 543–550; and N.P. Gregersen. 1996. Young Drivers' Overestimation of Their Own Skill: An Experiment on the Relation Between Training Strategy and Skill. *Accident Analysis & Prevention.* 28 (2). pp. 243–250

[64] N. P. Gregersen, A. Nyberg, and H. Y. Berg. 2003. Accident Involvement Among Learner Drivers—An Analysis of the Consequences of Supervised Practice. *Accident Analysis & Prevention.* 35 (5). pp. 725–730.

[65] T. Prabhakar, S. H. V. Lee, and R. F. S. Job. 1996. Risk Taking, *Optimism Bias and Risk Utility in Young Drivers.* In L. St. John, ed. In Proceedings of the Road Safety Research and Enforcement Conference. pp. 61–68. Sydney, Australia: Roads & Traffic Authority of NSW.

[66] C. Sakashita. 2007. *Comparing Provisional and Unrestricted License Holders on Speeding Offences and Crash Rates.* In Proceedings of the Australasian Road Safety Research Policing and Education Conference. Melbourne, Australia. 17–19 October.

The problem is compounded by the human capacity to misjudge risk.

Psychological Misjudgment of Risk

While it may be hoped that the impetus to speed will be significantly countered by the risk of a serious crash, the internal psychological dismissal of personal risk operates powerfully against the expected safety-inducing effects of crash risk. This dismissal of personal risk constitutes the second psychosocial structure (along with the positives associated with speed) sustaining unsafe travel speed as a cultural norm in most countries.[67]

Three closely related psychological mechanisms constitute this wall. First, **optimism bias** is the systematic psychological bias that we generally expect to have better lives than our peers. We expect that our futures will contain more positive events (being successful, winning an award, or having a long happy relationship) and fewer negative events (cancer, fired from work, early heart attack, or causing a serious car crash) than the average for our peers.[68] This bias has been found in studies across many countries.[69]

Second, **driver overconfidence** is a related phenomenon: most drivers believe that they are better and safer than average drivers. This too has been identified in many studies, in many countries.[70] For example, a study in Australia found that most drivers thought they were better than average, while only 2.1% thought that they were worse than average. These are psychological biases; most of us cannot be better, safer, healthier, wealthier, and happier than average.[71] Overall, the average for the community has to be average.

Third, **personal experience** forms part of the basis of optimism. In the case of driving, the errors of drivers around us are visible and often noted (including the common practice of referring to such drivers as idiots or similar terms), whereas our own errors are excused or even undetected by ourselves. Thus, we see ourselves as making fewer errors than others. Our personal experiences also dismiss personal risk. For example, many drivers will say that they have been speeding regularly for (insert almost any number) years, or months for young drivers, and have not killed themselves or anyone else. This invites one of two conclusions, with both supporting a view that speeding is safe *for me*: (i) the risks are exaggerated by road safety advocates as my experience demonstrates; and (ii) the risks of speeding may exist, but my experience shows that these risks do not apply to me, further supporting driver overconfidence.

The critical relevance of these biases is that they powerfully influence precaution-adoption (such as sticking to the speed limit) versus risk-taking (such as speeding).[72] Drivers who view themselves as better than others, and more skilled, safer, and less likely to cause a serious crash, are less likely to see their own speeding as a risk, or the chance of causing a serious crash as being a significant issue for them. So for most drivers the risk of crashing does not stop speeding, and promoting the risk of crashing does not help against these deep psychological defenses.

---

[67] Even those who stick to the speed limit are driving above safe system speed levels in many countries, because speed limits are typically set above safe system speeds. Safe systems speeds are described in J. Truong et al. 2022. Utilising Human Crash Tolerance to Design an Interim and Ultimate Safe System for Road Safety. *Sustainability*. 14 (6). p. 3491.

[68] N.D. Weinstein. 1980. Unrealistic Optimism About Future Life Events. *Journal of Personality and Social Psychology*. 39 (5). pp. 806–820.

[69] F. J. Chua and R. F. S. Job. 1999. Event-Specific Versus Unitary Causal Accounts of Optimism Bias. *Journal of Behavioral Medicine*. 22. pp. 457–491; N. Harre and C. G. Sibley. 2007. Explicit and Implicit Self-Enhancement Biases in Drivers and Their Relationship to Driving Violations and Crash-Risk Optimism. *Accident Analysis & Prevention*. 39 (6). pp. 1155–1161.

[70] J R. Dalziel and R. F. S. Job. 1997. Motor Vehicle Accidents, Fatigue, and Optimism Bias in Taxi Drivers. *Accident Analysis & Prevention*. 29. pp. 489–494; R. F. S. Job. 1990. The Application of Learning Theory to Driving Confidence: The Effect of Age and the Impact of Random Breath Testing. *Accident Analysis & Prevention*. 22. pp. 97–107; and O. Svenson. 1981. Are We All Less Risky and More Skillful than Our Fellow Drivers? *Acta Psychologica*. 47 (2). pp. 143–148.

[71] B. A. Jonah. 1986. Accident Risk and Risk-Taking Behavior Among Young Drivers. *Accident Analysis & Prevention*. 18. pp. 255–271; and T. Prabhakar, S. H. V. Lee, and R. F. S. Job. 1996. *Risk Taking, Optimism Bias and Risk Utility in Young Drivers*. In L. St. John, ed. In Proceedings of the Road Safety Research and Enforcement Conference. pp.61–68. Sydney, Australia: Roads & Traffic Authority of NSW.

[72] N. D. Weinstein. 1988. The Precaution Adoption Process. *Health Psychology*. 7 (4). p. 355.

Why Is Deterrence So Effective for Road Safety?

The problem for road safety is that the promotion of speed creates a motivation to speed, and the above psychological mechanisms eliminate the belief in the risks of a serious crash as a motivation not to speed. This is the reason for the proven outcome that the threat of enforcement is more effective in changing behavior than the threat of a serious crash and death.[73] This result may seem counterintuitive: surely, being killed or seriously injured in a crash is profoundly more serious than being caught and fined by police? The outcome here is not logical, but rather psychological. People simply do not believe that they will be killed or seriously injured in a crash, or if they accept it, then this risk it is due to "other bad drivers." However, people do believe that they might be caught by police or a camera and fined, with many countries having other penalties as well. This means that there can be extraordinary life-saving successes when general deterrence and enforcements are in place.[74]

B. Maximizing the Benefits of Enforcement and the Power of General Deterrence

We know that enforcement works, why it works, and that many alternative ways of changing road user behavior do not work. So, how do we make enforcement as effective as possible? Effective enforcement creates deterrence, the process of discouraging and thereby reducing the occurrence of relevant behaviors through actual or threatened consequences. From a large body of scientific evidence and experience of best practice, several features can be identified as improving the effectiveness of enforcement.

General and Specific Deterrence

Enforcement can work via two distinct mechanisms:

- by changing the behavior of a road user who is caught and fined, or otherwise punished, such as through license loss or vehicle impoundment—this is **specific deterrence**, or deterrence specific to each road user who is caught;[75] and
- by changing the behaviors of road users who have not been caught through the threat of being caught—**general deterrence**, or deterrence that is general across many road users.[76]

The concept of general deterrence, and to a lesser extent, specific deterrence, is vital for appreciating best practice across all aspects of enforcement.

Of these two mechanisms, general deterrence is much more powerful for road safety and indeed for much policing and enforcement activity, primarily because it can influence a huge number of people, whereas specific deterrence relies on catching everyone, which does not happen. Because general deterrence is the most important mechanism for improving road user behavior, it is critical that enforcement and associated processes focus on it.

Features That Create Better General and Specific Deterrence

The most effective enforcement generates the threat or fear of detection and penalties in many people. This general deterrence is improved by maximizing the **reality and perception** that offenses are:

- likely to be detected (the perceived risk of apprehension factor),
- punished with consequences that are unavoidable (the certainty factor),

---

[73] R. Phillips, P. Ulleberg, and T. Vaa. 2011. Meta-Analysis of the Effect of Road Safety Campaigns on Accidents. *Accident Analysis & Prevention.* 43 (3). pp. 1204–1218.

[74] R. F. S. Job, T. Prabhakar, and S. H. V. Lee. 1997. *The Long Term Benefits of Random Breath Testing in NSW (Australia): Deterrence and Social Disapproval of Drink-Driving.* In C. Mercier-Guyon, ed. In Proceedings of the 14th International Conference on Alcohol, Drugs and Traffic Safety. Annecy, France. pp. 841–848.

[75] *Specific deterrence* is deterrence of unwanted behaviors in specific offenders achieved by catching and punishing those offenders. This relies on the punishment being sufficient to deter, and that the punishment is unavoidable, and will be applied soon.

[76] *General deterrence* refers to the deterrence of unwanted behaviors, such as speeding, in the general population without necessarily catching each person. General deterrence is based on the beliefs of people that they are likely to be caught for a specific offense, that the punishment is significant (enough to deter), and that the punishment is unavoidable, and will be applied soon. These beliefs can be achieved through having effective enforcement and judicial systems as well as through promoting/advertising these features and punishments to the public. Various features of enforcement make this more likely to occur.

- punished with penalties that are sufficient to genuinely deter people from that behavior (the severity factor), and
- punished swiftly, through penalties that must be paid or are applied soon after the offense (the swiftness factor).[77]

Communications and campaigns show that these features are more effective in changing behavior than crash risk-based campaigns. For best-practice general deterrence campaign development, research is required to identify which of these features is least believed, which will identify likely areas of improvement.

Specific deterrence is also maximized by these factors. Specific deterrence provides additional opportunities, including medical or therapeutic interventions for people with alcohol or drug dependence, and applying penalties that make re-offending (or driving at all) much more physically difficult, e.g., through license loss and vehicle impoundment or immobilization.

Enforcement of behaviors after a crash (especially a serious crash) should result in stronger penalties than the same offense without a crash. This is appropriate based on the harm created. However, the psychological factors described show that post-crash enforcement is weak in the creation of general deterrence because drivers are overconfident and do not expect that their risky behavior will lead to a crash. Because having such a crash is seen as highly unlikely, the risk of detection (and application of these more serious penalties) is also seen as highly unlikely. The first requirement for general deterrence is not met. Thus, laws and penalties following crashes should not be relied upon as a mechanism of general deterrence, meaning that other enforcement mechanisms are needed. However, with jail sentences or other barriers to behavior such as vehicle impoundment, these laws can still be valuable for specific deterrence.

The processes required to maximize general deterrence are presented in Figure 2, which provides important practical guidance.

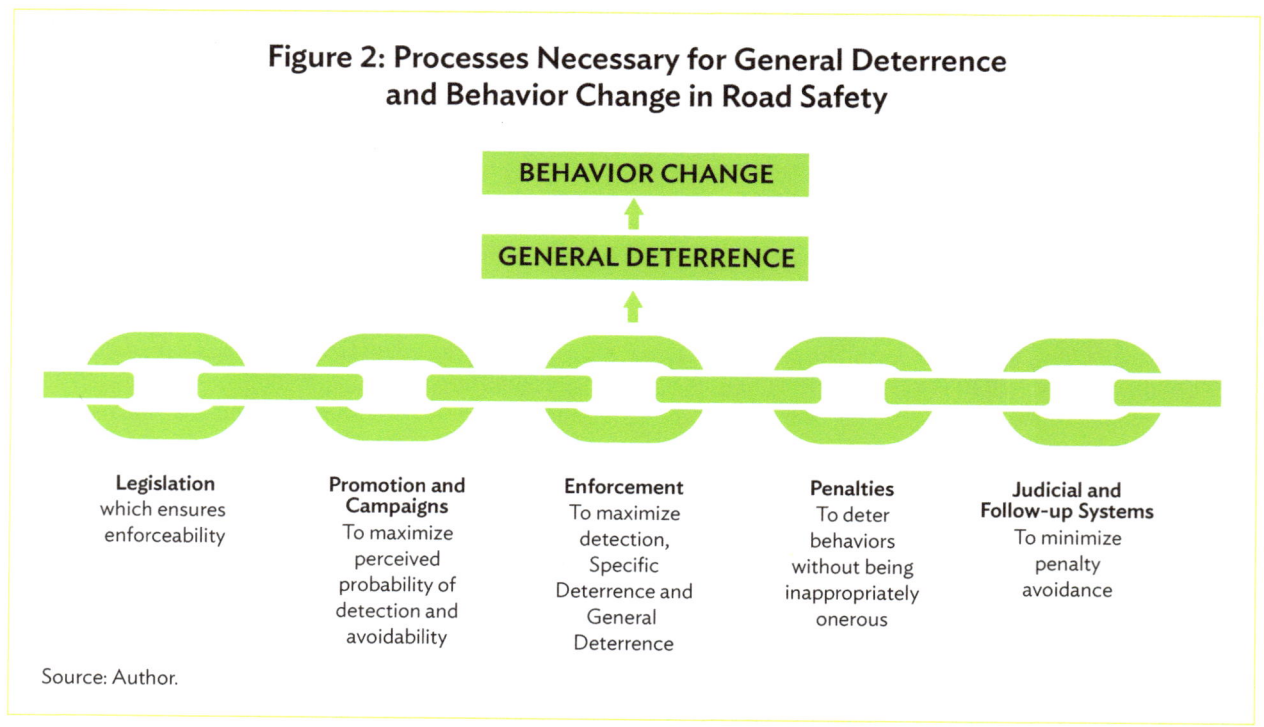

Figure 2: Processes Necessary for General Deterrence and Behavior Change in Road Safety

Source: Author.

[77] C. Sakashita et al. 2021. *A Guide to the Use of Penalties to Improve Road Safety.* Geneva: Global Road Safety Partnership.

A common but ineffective approach to behavior change is to focus on particular links or processes because they are easier to fix. For example, many LMIC governments, when faced with a lack of effective behavior change, opt for increasing the penalties, because this is within the control of the government to do. This may be useful if penalties are the weakest link, but often this is not the case. It is critical to appreciate that like a chain, the total system is only as strong as the weakest link. In the case of penalties, it is also important to consider the feasibility of people paying the penalty.[78] The weakest link approach has powerful practical consequences:

- through the collection and analysis of relevant data and information, the weakest link(s) must be identified and strengthened;
- spending resources on improving the already strongest links is ineffective; and
- there is no in-principle method for determining which process or link each country should focus on for improvement.

C. What Works in Behavior Change

Police enforcement is the mainstay of enforcement of road safety. The advantage of police enforcement is that the offender knows almost immediately that they face a penalty, because police stop them on the road at the time, rather than a penalty arriving later in the mail or by text message. Evidence shows that police enforcement reduces crashes. Increased speed enforcement is associated with reduced average driving speeds and number of speeding offenses (and thus crashes). The BCR of stationary speed enforcement is estimated to be between 3:1 and 12:1.

Good practice advice includes:

- adopting a zero tolerance approach to enforcing speed, which in practice means low tolerance on speeds before a penalty is applied, e.g., in the Australian state of Victoria, a speeding offense and penalty are applied to a driver at just 3 km/h above the posted speed limit);[79]
- ensuring that police efforts are focused on the most effective locations, times of day, and days of the week. The best predictive policing, or intelligence-based targeting of enforcement, comes from using both hot spot (blackspot) crash-based data and risk modeling, which also considers terrain and the risk of the offense;[80]
- preparing enforcement plans with annual targets for enforcement and compliance in the areas of speeding, drink and drug driving, and seat belt use (footnote 82);
- implementing a demerit system that includes a set of fixed penalties for minor speeding (and other) offenses, or include speeding offenses in penalty point systems where they exist (footnote 82).

Fixed-speed cameras are cameras that are not moved and so enforce speed at a set location. This is effective for treating a particular high-risk location, but generally does not result in a broader reduction of speeding and speed-related crashes away from the camera location, because drivers slow for the camera and speed up again once they are past it.[81] The Cochrane Library review concluded that the "consistency of reported reductions in speed and crash outcomes across all studies show that speed cameras are a worthwhile intervention for reducing the number of road traffic injuries and deaths."[82]

---

[78] An appropriate level of penalty must be uncomfortable to pay in order to deter. However, increasing penalties to a level at which even those who can access a vehicle to drive it cannot afford to pay the penalty will not be helpful. Thus, the appropriate level of penalty will vary across countries.
[79] ETSC. 2020. Enforcement in the EU – Vision 2020. Brussels.
[80] S. Sieveneck and C. Sutter. 2021. Predictive Policing in the Context of Road Traffic Safety: A Systematic Review and Theoretical Considerations. *Transportation Research Interdisciplinary Perspectives.* 11. 100429.
[81] R. F. S. Job. 2013. *Overcoming Barriers to Effective Management of Speeding.* Paper prepared for Australasian College of Road Safety Seminar: A Culture of Speed. Canberra. 14 March.
[82] C. Wilson et al. 2010. Speed Cameras for the Prevention of Road Traffic Injuries and Deaths. *Cochrane Database of Systematic Reviews.* 6 October. Art. No.: CD004607.

They are rated as highly effective by the World Bank (footnote 16), and other reviews of international evidence also conclude that they are effective, as well as delivering high BCRs, at around 14:1.[83] In Australia, fixed speed cameras in the state of NSW delivered substantial reductions in speeding and mean speed, as well as reducing fatal crashes by 90% and injury crashes by 20% along the roads treated with cameras.[84] This also highlights that the benefits of reducing speeding are much larger than could occur if the estimated involvement of speeding if the crash data record of speeding involvement in fatal crashes, 40%, was correct. In Poland, reducing the number of cameras in operation increased the number of crashes,[85] while in other countries, the success of fixed speed cameras has also been shown: including Finland,[86] Spain,[87] Norway,[88] and the US.[89]

The evidence in low- to middle-income countries meanwhile is also solid. In Thailand, a fixed speed camera program on a major urban road resulted in vehicle speed decreasing by 9.6% and a decline in of crashes by 5.8%, injuries by 7.7%, and fatalities by 34.3%.[90] In Brazil, an evaluation of lower speed limits and speed cameras found that the safety benefits were larger when both lower limits and cameras were present.[91]

Mobile speed cameras can be moved around the road network to enforce speeding at any location and are rated as highly effective by the World Bank (footnote 16). In New Zealand, a mix of visible and covert speed enforcement have been shown to work more effectively than having either alone.[92] In the Netherlands, mobile radar resulted in large reductions in injuries and serious injuries, including a broader influence to roads on which enforcement did not occur.[93] In Canada, mobile speed cameras led to reduced speeding and a 17% reduction in fatalities;[94] Australia, strong effects on casualty crashes was found on the same day as enforcement when high levels of mobile radar publicity accompanied mobile radar enforcement operations involving both overt and covert enforcement.[95]

Evidence-based good practice advice includes:

- a mix of visible and hidden speed enforcement works more effectively than having either alone;
- hidden enforcement should be publicized to the community weeks before it starts to ensure that drivers know it exists, and thus maximize compliance;
- randomized scheduling of mobile camera operations to enforcement sites improves safety benefits;

---

[83] R. F. S. Job and W. Mbugua. 2020. Road Crash Trauma, Climate Change, Pollution and the Total Costs of Speed: Six Graphs that Tell the Story. Washington, DC: Global Road Safety Facility, World Bank.

[84] R. F. S. Job. 2012. *Applications of Safe System Principles in Australia*. Paper prepared for the 2012 Australasian Road Safety Research, Policing and Education Conference. Wellington, New Zealand. October.

[85] J. Chmielewski. 2019. *Road Safety in Poland Three Years After Limiting the Number of Speed Controls*. In IOP Conference Series: Materials Science and Engineering. 603 (2). p. 022071.

[86] K. Shin, S. P. Washington, and I. van Schalkwyk. 2009. Evaluation of the Scottsdale Loop 101 Automated Speed Enforcement Demonstration Program. *Accident Analysis & Prevention*. 41 (3). pp. 393–403.

[87] K. Pérez et al. 2007. Reducing Road Traffic Injuries: Effectiveness of Speed Cameras in an Urban Setting. *American Journal of Public Health*. 97 (9). pp. 1632–1637.

[88] J. Luoma, R. Rajamäki, and M. Malmivuo. 2012. Effects of Reduced Threshold of Automated Speed Enforcement on Speed and Safety. *Transportation Research Part F: Traffic Psychology and Behavior*. 15 (3). pp. 243–248.

[89] A. Høye. 2015. Safety Effects of Fixed Speed Cameras—An Empirical Bayes Evaluation. *Accident Analysis & Prevention*. 82. pp. 263–269.

[90] P. Tankasem et al. 2019. Automated Speed Control on Urban Arterial Road: An Experience from Khon Kaen City, Thailand. *Transportation Research Interdisciplinary Perspectives*. 1. 100032.

[91] A. Ang, P. Christensen, and R. Vieira. 2020. Should Congested Cities Reduce Their Speed Limits? Evidence from São Paulo, Brazil. *Journal of Public Economics*. 184. 104155.

[92] M. D. Keall, L. J. Povey, and W. J. Frith. 2001. The Relative Effectiveness of a Hidden Versus a Visible Speed Camera Programme. *Accident Analysis & Prevention*. 33 (2). pp. 277–284.

[93] C. Goldenbeld and I. van Schagen. 2005. The Effects of Speed Enforcement with Mobile Radar on Speed and Accidents: An Evaluation Study on Rural Roads in the Dutch Province Friesland. *Accident Analysis & Prevention*. 37 (6). pp. 1135–1144.

[94] G. Chen et al. 2000. Evaluation of Photo Radar Program in British Columbia. *Accident Analysis & Prevention*. 32 (4). pp. 517–526.

[95] A. Delaney, K. Diamantopoulou, and M. Cameron. 2003. MUARC's Speed Enforcement Research: Principles Learnt and Implications for Practice. *Report No. 200*. Monash University Accident Research Center.

- the use of many enforcement sites to reduce the predictability of enforcement;[96] and
- most cameras should not be indicated with warning signs, however general warning signage that cameras are in use has the benefit of increasing reminders to drivers, thus increasing general deterrence.

Mobile speed cameras are a key additional tool to use in conjunction with fixed speed cameras. While fixed cameras are predictable, they are effective in treating so-called blackspots. Most fatal crashes however do not occur at known blackspots, e.g., in the Australian state of NSW, all the fatal crash locations in one year compared with the previous year showed only a 12% overlap. This means that even treating every fatal crash location from the whole year (not just blackspots) would only address 12% of next years' fatalities. Network-wide speed enforcement help to address the remaining 88%. For an example of good practice in the CAREC region, see Box 3.

Average speed camera technology involves using two or more connected cameras along a section of road. Also known as point-to-point or section control cameras, they take a photo, record the exact time of the photo being taken, and collect vehicle registration data from vehicles at each point and match them using automatic number plate recognition technology. The average speed of a vehicle between two cameras is then calculated. If the average speed of a vehicle is found to exceed the legal posted speed limit for that road section (plus any enforcement tolerance), images and offense data are transmitted to a central processing unit (or back office) from the local processor via a communication network, where human verification occurs to assess the validity of detected infringements.[97]

The powerful advantage of average speed cameras is that speed can be enforced over long distances, not just at a camera location. Reviews provide strong evidence supporting the safety benefits of average speed cameras (footnote 97). In Poland, for instance, average speed cameras produce stronger reductions in speed than fixed cameras.[98] In the Republic of Korea, analysis shows average speed cameras result in drivers reducing their speeds,[99] while in Italy, the

Box 3: Good Practice in Automated Speed Enforcement in Mongolia

Mongolia has a significant speed camera program covering both urban and non-urban roads. The national police operate a speed camera program of two or three mobile speed cameras in each of 21 regions.

In addition, the Ulaanbaatar Traffic Control Center operates programs of three red-light cameras, two mobile speed cameras, and many more fixed speed cameras, as well as lane enforcement cameras.

Over the first 7 years of the program in Ulaanbaatar

- only 7% of vehicle registration numbers could not be recognized by the cameras (due to lighting, angle of the view, etc);
- on average, more than 358,000 infringements per year were issued by all enforcement cameras; and
- 84.1% of fines have been paid.

These numbers are sufficient to achieve significant deterrence.

Source: Prevention Division of Transport Police Department and Transport Development, and the Ulaanbaatar Traffic Control Center.

---

[96] M. Cameron and S. Newstead. 2021. Increasing the Effectiveness of Mobile Speed Cameras on Rural Roads in Victoria based on Crash Reductions from Operations in Queensland. *Journal of Road Safety*. 32 (2). pp. 16–21.

[97] D. W. Soole, B.C. Watson, and J. J. Fleiter. 2013. Effects of Average Speed Enforcement on Speed Compliance and Crashes: A Review of the Literature. *Accident Analysis & Prevention*. 54. pp. 46–56.

[98] R. Ziolkowski. 2019. Effectiveness of Automatic Section Speed Control System Operating on National Roads in Poland. *Promet-Traffic & Transportation*. 31 (4). pp. 435–442.

[99] J. Shim et al. 2020. Evaluation of Section Speed Enforcement System Using Empirical Bayes Approach and Turning Point Analysis. *Journal of Advanced Transportation*. 2020.

cameras reduced crashes by 32%.[100] In Australia, BCRs for average speed enforcement were between 7.4 and 12.5. For Belgium, average speed cameras reduced speeding by 76%, yielding a dramatic and predicted safety benefit.[101]

Because red-light disobedience is commonly the result of speeding, **red-light cameras** may be seen as a form of speed enforcement. In addition, **combined speed and red-light cameras** enforce drivers who speed or disobey red lights or both. The logic behind these combined cameras is that the red-light function reduces red-light running, while the speed function reduces speeding, and in particular drivers speeding up to get through the location before the light turns red (Figure 5).

Literature reviews of evidence find substantial safety benefits of red-light cameras.[102] In Belgium, combined red-light speed cameras resulted in significant reduction in serious crashes.[103] In the US, a large-scale evaluation showed that rates of fatal red-light running crashes were 21% lower in cities with cameras than in cities without. After red-light cameras were turned off in some cities however, these fatal crashes increased.[104]

Red light camera in Astana, Kazakhstan (photo by Soames Job Job).

Other Examples

A study of red-light cameras in Hong Kong, China found that increasing penalties resulted in a decrease in red-light disobedience.[105] In Jordan, red-light and speed cameras substantially reduced crashes and severe crashes (injury and fatal crashes),[106] while in Colombia, combined red-light speed cameras led to a reduction of 19.2% in all crashes and a 24.7% reduction in injury and fatal crashes at camera locations. This effect was also found at other intersections.[107]

---

[100] A. Montella et al. 2015. Effects on Speed and Safety of Point-to-Point Speed Enforcement Systems: Evaluation on the Urban Motorway A56 Tangenziale di Napoli. *Accident Analysis & Prevention*. 75. pp. 164–178.

[101] E. De Pauw et al. 2014. Automated Section Speed Control on Motorways: An Evaluation of the Effect on Driving Speed. *Accident Analysis & Prevention*. 73. pp. 313–322.

[102] A. Aeron-Thomas and S. Hess. 2005. Red-Light Cameras for the Prevention of Road Traffic Crashes. *Cochrane Database of Systematic Reviews*. 2; and A. F. Llau and N.U. Ahmed. 2014. The Effectiveness of Red-Light Cameras in the United States—A Literature Review. Traffic Injury Prevention. 15 (6). pp. 542–550.

[103] E. De Pauw et al. 2014. To Brake or to Accelerate? Safety Effects of Combined Speed and Red Light Cameras. *Journal of Safety Research*. 50. pp. 59–65.

[104] W. Hu and J. Cicchino. 2017. Effects of Turning On and Off Red Light Cameras on Fatal Crashes in Large US Cities. *Journal of Safety Research*. 61. pp. 141–148.

[105] N. Sze et al. 2011. Is a Combined Enforcement and Penalty Strategy Effective in Combating Red Light Violations? An Aggregate Model of Violation Behavior in Hong Kong. *Accident Analysis & Prevention*. 43 (1). pp. 265–271.

[106] H. Naghawi, B. Al Qatawneh, and R. Al Louzi. 2018. Evaluation of Automated Enforcement Program in Amman. *Periodica Polytechnica Transportation Engineering*. 46 (4). pp. 201–206.

[107] D. M. Martínez-Ruíz et al. 2019. Impact Evaluation of Camera Enforcement for Traffic Violations in Cali, Colombia, 2008–2014. *Accident Analysis & Prevention*. 125. pp.267–274.

Promotion of Enforcement Versus Promotion of Crash Risk and Consequences

Road safety campaigns on speeding mainly focus on two types of messages: (i) explaining or showing the risk of a serious crash caused by speeding, and (ii) explaining or showing the risk of being caught by enforcement. For the reasons explained earlier, explaining or showing the risk of enforcement works much better to change driver behavior.

A review and meta-analysis of evidence from many countries shows that campaigns with enforcement messages are more effective, while campaigns based on crash-risk messages are of limited value. Many examples of the life-saving benefits of introducing speed enforcement involved campaigns warning that the changes in enforcement were coming soon. Thus, many of the studies above are really evaluations of the combined effects of the right campaign and the enforcement.

Graduated Licensing Schemes

Another area of strong enforcement of speeding relates to graduated licensing schemes (GLS). In GLS, instead of the novice driver passing a test and being able to drive following all the usual laws, the driver has a series of tests over time, with each one allowing them more freedom, until a full license is reached. One substantial advantage of this is that extra restrictions are possible for particularly risky behaviors. For example, instead of having the normal 0.05 blood alcohol concentration limit, the novice driver initially has a zero limit, and instead of a fine, the novice driver may lose their license for any speeding.

Figure 3 provides a good GLS example from the Australian state of NSW, where the novice driver must pass four advancing tests to obtain their final full license. At each stage prior to reaching this point, the driver has extra restrictions placed on their driving, which can be enforced because the driver is required to display the L, P1, or P2 sign on the vehicle they are driving. For example, learner drivers have the extra restriction of only driving with an experienced driver supervising their driving in the car. Most relevant for speeding, Provisional 1 (P1) drivers must drive at a maximum speed of 90 km/h even on roads with a higher posted speed limit, and lose their license for 3 months for any level of speeding in addition to the penalties applied to other drivers. Provisional 2 (P2) drivers have a maximum allowed speed of 100 km/h even if the road is limited to 110 km/h, and lose their license for any two speeding offenses in addition to the usual penalties.

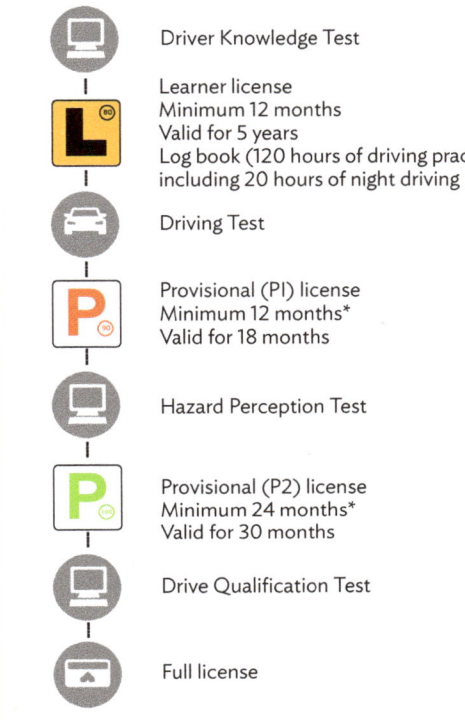

Figure 3: The Graduated Licensing Scheme from New South Wales, Australia

- Driver Knowledge Test
- Learner license
  Minimum 12 months
  Valid for 5 years
  Log book (120 hours of driving practice including 20 hours of night driving
- Driving Test
- Provisional (P1) license
  Minimum 12 months*
  Valid for 18 months
- Hazard Perception Test
- Provisional (P2) license
  Minimum 24 months*
  Valid for 30 months
- Drive Qualification Test
- Full license

Source: New South Wales Centre for Road Safety.

The license loss penalty was added to the GLS in this example after the GLS was operating, allowing for an evaluation of the effects of this change on P1 drivers. The before and after comparison showed that the addition of a license-loss penalty for any speeding resulted in a 34% reduction in fatal crashes involving P1 drivers, with the largest reduction being for speeding crashes.

D. Prioritizing Behavior Change Opportunities

The psychology of behavior change in road safety has vital practical applications supported by the evidence of what works in this field. Recommendations taking these into account include:

- Employ the psychology of road safety, human behavior, and human misjudgment of risk covered here to explain why many recommendations that we might expect to work actually do not work, and to explain why enforcement changes behavior. This also highlights the need for road safety decisions to be evidence based.
- Shift from education to a focus on enforcement and deterrence.
- The most effective enforcement generates the threat (fear) of detection and penalties in a large portion of the targeted population, which is known as general deterrence. Communications and campaigns taking this into account are recommended, with details of messages to be determined based on research of current beliefs.
- The chain of processes required to increase general deterrence includes legislation, promotion and campaigns, enforcement, penalties, and judicial and follow-up processes. Like a chain, the total system is only as strong as the weakest link, which must be identified and strengthened; spending resources on improving the strongest links is ineffective. There is no standard method for determining which process or link each country should focus for improvement but the weakest link(s) can be identified through the collection and analysis of relevant data and information.
- Effectively enforcing speeding will involve choosing from among the following, based on the particular circumstances faced:
    » police enforcement,
    » fixed speed cameras,
    » mobile speed cameras, and
    » combined red-light and speed cameras.
- Ensure that enforcement is a balanced mix of overt (visible) and covert (hidden) enforcement.
- Apply all the usual penalties to speeding when detected by cameras.
- Many serious crashes occur at night, yet speed enforcement cameras in some CAREC countries are not able to operate at night; improved technology and resourcing for nighttime enforcement is recommended.
- Enforcement and penalties should be strongly publicized to the community. Campaigns should have the following features:
    » Be based on surveys of community attitudes and beliefs to ensure that the publicity is relevant, e.g., publicising information about which the community is already well aware is not helpful.
    » New enforcement processes, expanded enforcement, or additional penalties should be publicized weeks in advance of the changes occurring, so that people are warned and have time to change habits before the changes occur.
    » For behavior change, publicity should not be based on crash risks or consequences. The evidence shows that this is ineffective even though people will report that they approve of these campaigns and believe that they work.
- Laws and penalties following crashes should not be relied upon as a mechanism of general deterrence, meaning that other enforcement mechanisms are needed. However, with jail sentences or other barriers to behavior such as vehicle impoundment, these laws can be valuable for specific deterrence.
- Create a GLS and include additional restrictions on speed and additional penalties for speeding for novice drivers.
- Maintain data to evaluate speeding interventions. If crash data are not reliable and comprehensive, then before and after surveys of speeds can be sufficient, and should be collected even if crash data are reliable. Speed surveys combined with the information in Module VII can be used to calculate expected reductions in deaths and injuries.

V. Reducing Speed Through Modal Shift and City Planning

The motivation for speeding can be reduced in urban contexts through improved city planning and modal shift. This is a deeply neglected areas of public infrastructure planning, building, and policy, which has been driven by motorist demands and LMICs following poor models from other countries.

A. Modal Shift

Modal shift refers to moving people from one transport mode (in this case, motorized road use) to other transport modes, e.g. metro/subway, bus rapid transport (BRT) systems on closed road sections, water transport. For rural transport, modal shift might be to rail, air, or water transport. Despite the extensive publicity given to sensational events in other forms of transport (such as planes crashing and boats sinking with many lives lost), these events are relatively rare, whereas globally well over 3,000 people are killed on roads each day. Other modes of transport are dramatically safer than road transport, with 97% of all transport deaths occurring during road transport.[108] The following policies and actions are effective in generating the shift to safer modes of transport:

- Building, expanding, or improving effective alternative options to road transport, e.g., metro, rail, and water transport such as ferries, air, and BRT systems.
- Implementing policies that ensure these alternative transport systems are highly cost competitive through low fares and costs for moving goods, combined with policies that increase the costs of private motor transport (such as via fuel levies or road use charges for vehicles, especially heavy vehicles). Sound policy is to allow the additional fees and/or levies collected on road transport to be used to subsidize fares on the other transport modes.
- Implementing policies that ensure these alternative transport systems are faster than private motorized road transport through reducing increasing road space for motorized public transport, e.g., by adding dedicated (and physically protected) bicycle lanes, wider footpaths, and BRT systems in the middle of existing multi-lane roads; setting traffic signals to give priority at intersections to BRT over other traffic; as supported by safety and economic benefits, setting low speed limits for motorized road transport. Such policies are often referred to as road diets (see following discussion).
- Improving public transport services, which increases use, thus reducing not only road safety risk, but also air pollution and greenhouse gas emissions.[109]

Road Diets

A road diet refers to a deliberate process of reducing the number of travel lanes and/or narrowing travel lanes on a road to utilize the space for other uses and travel modes (such as cycling or walking). It should also include a policy of not expanding roads due to demand, but instead providing safer, more environmentally friendly mass transit options (such as BRT) and further incentivizing use of public transport by not providing more road space for private motorized transport. Good-practice road safety cities in various countries are delivering safer, more livable cities through this process, e.g., Barcelona, New York, and London. Narrowing marked lanes or reducing available road space lowers speeds,[110] which incentivizes public transport and creates a more comfortable environment for all road users, including

---

[108] H. M. Gomez et al. 2017. Chapter 4: Safety. In Sustainable Mobility for All. 2017. *Global Mobility Report 2017: Tracking Sector Performance*. Washington, DC.

[109] International Transport Federation (ITF). 2023. How Improving Public Transport and Shared Mobility Can Reduce Urban Passenger Carbon Emissions. Paris.

[110] K. Fitzpatrick et al. 2001. Design Factors that Affect Driver Speed on Suburban Streets. *Transportation Research Record*. 1751 (1). pp. 18–25; M. Poch and F. Mannering. 1996. Negative Binomial Analysis of Intersection-Accident frequencies. *Journal of Transportation Engineering*. 122 (2). pp. 105-113; and O. Farouki and W. Nixion. 1976. The Effect of the Width of Suburban Roads on the Mean Free Speed of Cars. *Traffic Engineering and Control*. December. pp. 518–519.

pedestrians and cyclists. Many other benefits are also delivered, such as shorter pedestrians crossing times due to narrower roads; more space for additional safety features such as crash barriers and raised medians; reduced stormwater runoff; and increased livability, with more space for vegetation.

BRT systems, which absorb lanes from existing roads, reducing road space and slowing traffic to incentivize their use, are in effective use in CAREC countries, with lessons to be learned from them (Box 4).

B. Urban Planning

Urban planning has substantial influence on road safety via road use. Net serious crash risk is determined by the risk per kilometer of road travel times and the number of kilometers of driving undertaken. Thus, reducing the number of kilometers of road travel via better city planning is a valuable yet overlooked opportunity in road safety. In addition, urban planning has the potential to reduce the incentive to speed by reducing required travel

Box 4: Case Studies of Bus Rapid Transit Developments in the People's Republic of China and Pakistan

The People's Republic of China (PRC) was an early adopter of bus rapid transit (BRT) systems, with its first BRT placed in the road median in Kunming in 1999, followed by Beijing in 2004, Hangzhou in 2006, and, with increasing perceptions of efficacy, five more cities in 2008. Now BRT systems operate in many cities in the PRC, which is in part attributed to the needs of many large-population cities, and in part to Chinese mayors having greater independent discretion with regards to transportation planning and budgeting than is typical internationally. Pakistan has also adopted multiple BRT systems in major cities since the first BRT installation in Lahore in 2013. Research has found satisfaction and efficacy for the systems in Lahore, Multan, and Rawalpindi-Islamabad.

BRT systems are more affordable than metro systems, with global review studies indicating that appropriately designed and operated BRT systems also provide a high-quality transport service, comparable with rail and with faster implementation due to their ability to use existing road space. BRT systems can be an effective transportation opportunity for large low- to middle-income country cities due to these lower costs of implementation, and thus the lower fares required of users. BRT systems are increasingly common in Latin America, Asia, and Africa.

Analyses highlight lessons to be learned from the PRC's and Pakistan's BRT systems. The PRC's BRT systems often include high quality services to increase use; Pakistan's BRT systems show high levels of satisfaction with the BRT itself, but highlight the lack of effective transport to reach the BRT systems.

In Pakistan, population density, development volume, and land use for economic activities all increased after the BRT systems were operating; they could be further improved by addressing transit, walking, and security issues for women. Ridership could also be improved if lane design allowed for faster movement of BRT than other traffic with more dedicated lanes for BRT overtaking. Selective development of BRTs where demand is high would allow for fares to cover more of the operating costs, while station spacing can be increased to improve BRT speed and reliability, though this must be balanced with acceptable walking distances for users.

In the PRC, provision of bicycle parking facilities at BRT stations increases access for users, as exists in Guangzhou; public policy to incentivize use of BRTs through greater relative cost of other forms of motorized road transport.

Sources:

T. Deng, M. Ma, and J. Wang. 2013. Evaluation of Bus Rapid Transit Implementation: Current Performance and Progress. *Journal of Urban Planning and Development*. 139 (3). pp.226–234.
D.A. Hensher and T.F. Golob. 2008. Bus Rapid Transit Systems: A Comparative Assessment. *Transportation*. 35 (4). pp. 501–518.
A. Khan. 2021. Measuring Survey-Based Trip Satisfaction of Feeder Modes for Bus Rapid Transit in Rawalpindi Islamabad, Pakistan. *Urban and Regional Planning Review*. 8. pp. 147–164.
B.Z. Malik et al. 2020. Women's Mobility via Bus Rapid Transit: Experiential Patterns and Challenges in Lahore. *Journal of Transport & Health*. 17. p. 100834.
M. Nadeem et al. 2021. Does the Bus Rapid Transit System (BRTS) Meet the Citizens' Mobility Needs? Evaluating Performance for the Case of Multan, Pakistan. *Sustainability*. 13. p. 7314.
M. Nadeem, M. Matsuyuki, and S. Tanaka. 2023. Impact of Bus Rapid Transit in Shaping Transit-Oriented Development: evidence from Lahore, Pakistan. *Journal of Asian Architecture and Building Engineering*. pp. 3635-3648.

distances. For example, if shopping opportunities were not concentrated in a small number of centers but were more effectively distributed across residential areas, people would have less need to travel to shop. Similar logic applies for other activities, such as sports fields and entertainment venues. Detailed analyses show that this so-called "slow cities" approach is better for inhabitants' health in many ways.[111] Urban sprawl (i.e., low density, long blocks, and poor street connectivity) is directly related to poor road safety. For every 1% change toward a more compact and connected urban form, road crash fatality rates fall by 1.49% and pedestrian fatality rates by 1.47%–3.56%.[112]

A comparison of cities designed with urban sprawl and thus car dependency versus cities with high urban density reveals huge differences. For example, a comparison of Barcelona, Spain with Atlanta, US, shows stark differences. These two cities have similar population sizes, but Atlanta is spread over 26 times the land area of Barcelona, and each has very different transport modes and crash death rates (Table 1).

Land-use planning that increases the density of urban dwelling space and provides connection via safe, rapid transport systems, has been shown to provide the best safety and reduce public health burdens.[113] As well, reclaiming street space for footpaths, recreation, and café seating improves road safety and livability in cities.[114] In Latin America, one study found that each additional traffic lane increased the number of fatal crashes by 17%.[115]

C. Prioritizing Modal Shift and City Planning Opportunities

City planning, combined with road diets, multi-road user sensitive street design, and alternative transport options can greatly influence how people use streets, reduce the motivation to speed, and facilitate modal shift to safer transport than personal motorized road use. The right policy and infrastructure changes can reduce or eliminate conflicts between modes of transport and make it easier for people to understand

Table 1: Comparison of Atlanta, United States and Barcelona, Spain

City	Atlanta	Barcelona
Population	2.5 million	2.8 million
Land area	4,280 square kilometers	162 square kilometers
Traffic fatality rate (deaths per 100,000 inhabitants)	9.7	1.9
Transport mode: cars	77%	20%
Transport mode: Public transport	3%	33%
Transport mode: Bicycle	0%	12%
Transport mode: Walking	1%	35%

Source: C. Adriazola-Steil. 2015. *Saving Lives Through Vision Zero and Cities Safer by Design.* Washington, DC: World Resources Institute.

---

[111] S. Ball. 2015. Slow Cities. In W. K. D. Davies, ed. *Theme Cities: Solutions for Urban Problems.* Springer Dordrecht. pp. 563–585; and M. Çiçek, S. Ulu, and C. Uslay. 2019. The Impact of the Slow City Movement on Place Authenticity, Entrepreneurial Opportunity, and Economic Development. *Journal of Macromarketing.* 39 (4). pp. 400–414.

[112] R. Ewing, R. A. Schieber, and C. V. Zegeer. 2003. Urban Sprawl as a Risk Factor in Motor Vehicle Occupant and Pedestrian Fatalities. *American Journal of Public Health.* 93 (9): 1541–45.

[113] R. J. McClure et al. 2015. Simulating the Dynamic Effect of Land Use and Transport Policies on the Health of Populations. *American Journal of Public Health.* 105 (Suppl. 2): S223–S229.

[114] B. Welle. 2018. *Safe and Sustainable: A Vision and Guidance for Zero Road Deaths.* Washington, DC: World Resources Institute & Global Road Safety Facility.

[115] N. Duduta et al. 2015. Traffic Safety on Bus Priority Systems: Recommendations for Integrating Safety into the Planning, Design, and Operation of Major Bus Routes. Washington, DC: EMBARQ/World Bank Group.

how the space is divided or shared by different modes, which makes walking, cycling, and accessing public transport much safer and more appealing. Multiple benefits arise from lower speeds and less driving: improved road safety, reduced air and noise pollution, increased city livability, and increased economic growth. These often work as a combined set, and many LMICs have found that absorbing road space for BRT systems is an effective early step, including in the CAREC countries of Pakistan and the PRC.

Recommendations for Modal Shift and City Planning

Road safety stakeholders must work with city and land-use planners to increase the appreciation of their impacts on crash deaths and injuries and their opportunities to help manage speed as the key risk factor. Many proven steps are recommended, and these should be considered in combinations to ensure efficacy:

- Implement and/or expand BRT systems and absorb road space for these, rather than attempting to maintain the current number of lanes, noting the additional benefit that reducing the number of lanes directly improves road safety.
- Incentivize BRT use through:
    » policies that appropriately rebalance the costs of private motor transport versus BRT;
    » designs and priorities that ensure that the BRT system will get people to their destination in less time;
    » integrating BRT systems with transport options for people to reach them, including station designs that incorporate other transport modes and providing bicycle parking as appropriate; and
    » preventing motorcycle parking on footpaths, which both adds to crash risk for pedestrians who are forced to walk on the road, and incentivizes motorcycle transport (the most serious crash-risk prone of all transport) through convenience.
- Design cities for high urban density.
- Implement city planning that reduces the need for road transport.
- Reclaim street space for footpaths, recreation, and café seating to improve road safety and livability.
- Provide safe travel spaces for pedestrians, bicyclists, and motorcyclists, which can also reduce road space for cars—providing multiple benefits as a road diet initiative.
- Implement road diet policies.

Examples of effective road diet implementation facilitating safer walking, cycling, and e-mobility by absorbing motorized vehicle road space for cycle lanes and complete or wider pedestrian facilities, in Almaty, Kazakhstan.

VI. Delivering Improved Speed Management: Persuading and Managing Delivery of What Works

This module provides guidance on selecting the best actions that work for a particular municipality, state or country, and how to manage and deliver their implementation.

A. Selecting the Best Speed Management Actions

It is important that each jurisdiction chooses the most appropriate tools for their particular circumstances for implementation.[116]

Five criteria are of primary importance; each is discussed in the following.

1: What is the nature of the speeding problem in the jurisdiction?

Information should be collated to answer the following questions for a particular jurisdiction:

- Do the current speed limits provide safety for all road users? This can be assessed against best practice, e.g., 30 km/h zones for roads where pedestrians are somewhat common.
- How are speed limits set, and by whom?
- Is there a guide or standard for setting speed limits, and does it need to be changed?
- How strong is speed limit compliance? Speed surveys may be necessary to answer this, and should be conducted regularly in many representative locations (not at known speed enforcement locations) to monitor progress.
- How common is speed limiting infrastructure, is it well designed and working to suppress speeds, and visible? Are there good standards for these, including specifying the conditions under which they should be used, rather than leaving this to inconsistent judgements?

- What are the features of speeding:

  Who? (e.g, speeders' common age)
  Where?
  When?

This can be supplemented with data on speed-related serious crashes, but these data should be treated with great caution (because many speeding crashes are missed in crash data, as explained earlier) or corrected with the evidence-based correction factor explained earlier. Best practice in top-performing countries is to accept that crash data are flawed for speed involvement. Instead, speeding is regarded as a major issue where speeding occurs and where serious crashes occur, without these being connected in crash data.

2: What are the best interventions?

Judgement here is based on four criteria:

- The **road safety impact** of an intervention reflects its ability to reduce serious crashes, as identified in the examples given in Modules II–V.
- Based on evidence for the road safety and overall economic benefits of lower speeds, all interventions to lower speeds support sustainability. However, some interventions themselves are more **sustainable**, meaning that they are more able to continue to be effective without continuous resources and effort. For example, speed humps and raised platform crossings are highly sustainable, requiring occasional low-cost paint treatments, whereas enforcement requires continuous effort and resourcing, with significant risk that priorities change and enforcement is not sustained.

---

[116] This section is based on relevant evidence, the author's experience, and C. Sakashita. 2019. *Strategies to Tackle the Speed Issue for Road Safety in the Asia-Pacific Region.* Bangkok: UNESCAP.

- **Best value** refers to best BCR.
- **Safe system contribution** refers to the extent to which the intervention helps to deliver a road system that either physically prevents human error (such as speed limiting a vehicle to physically prevent speeding) or reduces crash forces without relying on road users to avoid mistakes.

BCRs for various speed management interventions. Before moving fully into this decision step, it is important to canvas the evidence on BCRs for each intervention, because these guide the crash cost savings to be achieved compared with the cost of implementation. If an intervention has a BCR of 4.0, the action is expected to deliver four times as much benefit as it costs to achieve the intervention. Figure 4 shows the BCRs for many types of speed management interventions, highlighting that powerful and cost-effective interventions do exist to manage speed. The BCRs in the figure highlight the overall economic gains from investing in speed management. For example, a BCR of 17 for lane-narrowing and speed humps reflects that every dollar, tenge, or yen spent will save 17 dollars, tenge, or yen in crash costs. Similarly, automated (camera) speed enforcement will save 14 dollars, tenge, or yen for each one spent. In addition, these BCRs are underestimates of the full benefits to be achieved, because they focus on crash costs and leave out the other benefits of managing speed, such as improved economic growth (see Module VII). It is challenging for CAREC governments to find investments with stronger returns that these, yet governments still tend to rely on ineffective interventions such as school education (with a BCR of 0, i.e., no return in crash savings at all). This must change.

Even more impressive is that for several speed managing interventions, the BCRs are stronger in LMICs than in HICs. For example, as shown in Figure 4, area-wide traffic calming delivers much higher BCRs (17:1 to over 30:1) in LMICs than in HICs, where the BCRs are around 3:1. This has not been assessed for all interventions, but is to be expected, especially for road design and engineering treatments that sustain their purpose without reliance on multiple other stakeholders in the system doing their part. Higher BCRs in LMICs arise even though road engineering treatments work in a similar way everywhere because:

- costs (especially labor costs) are generally lower to install interventions in LMICs;
- there are more crash costs in LMICs because crash death and injury are more common in LMICs;
- speed is currently not as well managed in LMICs as in HICs, so there is more room for improvement; and
- LMICs have higher proportions of vulnerable road user casualties, and thus for serious crashes speeds become more critical at lower levels.

Table 2 presents a summary of the best speed management interventions for potential use in the CAREC region.

3: What are the best interventions for each CAREC country?

For CAREC countries facing challenges in delivering effective regular enforcement across their entire road network, road engineering measures such as road humps, raised pedestrian facilities, and prominent gateway treatments are the most effective, sustained interventions for urban and low or moderate speed environments.

Table 3 shows the potential savings of crash deaths in each country with changes to speed limits (and ensuring compliance with those speed limits through road engineering treatments and enforcement) on urban and rural roads.

Compliance with speed limits is often weak in CAREC countries. For example, in the PRC, International Road Assessment Programme (iRAP) speed survey data indicate that speed limits are commonly exceeded: Tacheng Road has a 30 km/h limit and the mean speed is 32 km/h, but 15% of vehicles are speeding at 41 km/h or higher; for Shengxin North Road, the speed limit is 50 km/h and the mean speed is 46 km/h, but 15% of traffic is traveling at above 56 km/h; and Liuxiang Highway has a limit of 60 km/h and a mean speed of 60 km/h, but 15% of vehicles are traveling above 71 km/h. The common pattern is that, on average, drivers speed by a reasonably predictable amount above the limit. Here the 85th percentile speeds are 6, 11, and 11 km/h above the limits, reflecting that drivers who speed still consider the speed limit and tend to speed by a certain amount above the limit.

Effectively, this means that lowering speed limits by just 10 km/h with similar levels of compliance to those existing now will save huge numbers of deaths and serious injuries, as well as reducing economic losses.

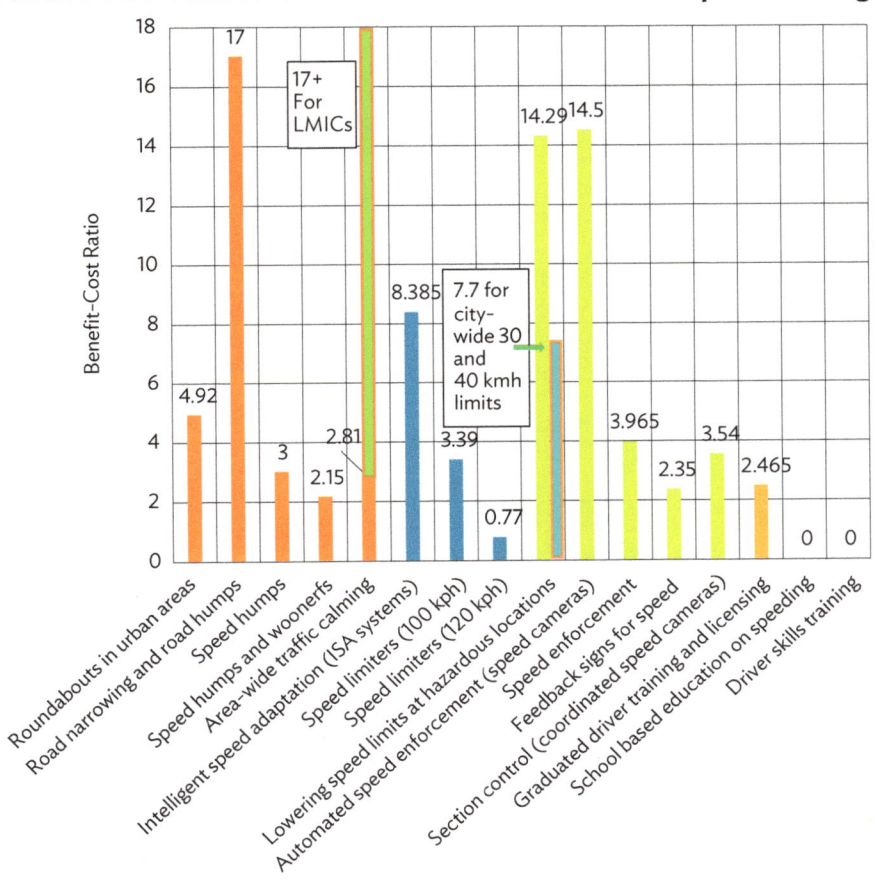

Figure 4: Benefit-Cost Ratios for Selected Interventions for Speed Management

km/h = kilometers per hour, LMICs = low- to middle-income countries.

Notes:
1. The bar for area-wide traffic calming in LMICs has been added here to the original, based on evidence presented by R.F.S. Job and L.W. Mbugua. 2020. *Road Crash Trauma, Climate Change, Pollution and the Total Costs of Speed: Six Graphs that Tell the Story.* GRSF Note 2020.1. Washington, DC: Global Road Safety Facility, World Bank.
2. Evidence shows that some speed management treatments yield higher benefit–cost ratios in LMICs than those often reported in higher-income countries. See D.R. Mohapatra. 2017. An Economic Evaluation of Feasibility of Non-Motorized Transport Facilities in Mombasa Town of Kenya. *In Economic and Financial Analysis of Infrastructure Projects, an Edited Volume.* pp 134–157. New Delhi: Educreation Publishing; and D.R. Mohapatra. 2017. Feasibility of Non-Motorized Transport Facilities in Addis Ababa City of Ethiopia: An Economic Analysis. *In Economic and Financial Analysis of Infrastructure Projects, an Edited Volume.* pp 184–204. New Delhi: Educreation Publishing. These papers found that implementing area-wide traffic calming in Mombasa in Kenya would yield a benefit–cost ratio (BCR) of 17.6, while in Addis Ababa in Ethiopia it would be 36.5.
3. The added bar in green reflects the much higher benefit–cost ratio for traffic calming in LMICs. Another study reported a BCR of 30 for area-wide traffic calming in Kampala, Uganda (United Nations Economic Commission for Africa & United Nations Economic Commission for Europe. 2018. Road Safety Performance Review Uganda. New York and Geneva: United Nations.
Similar treatments have BCRs of 1.9 to 3.68 for towns in Ireland and Greece (G. Yannis, P. Evgenikos, and E. Papadimitriou. 2008. *Best Practice for Cost-Effective Road Safety Infrastructure Investments.* Paris: Conference of European Directors of Roads.) These higher BCRS in LMICs are a result of higher numbers of serious crashes, allowing more benefits to be achieved with lower implementation costs. Other interventions, such as lower speed limits, without traffic calming, are less effective in LMICs where enforcement is less effective.
4. The extra bar in dark blue is the BCR for lowering urban speed limits to 30 km/h or 40 km/h. (S. Mandic et al. 2023. Approaches to Managing Speed in New Zealand's Capital. *Journal of Road Safety.* 34 (1).

Source: Additional data points added to information from R. F. S Job and L. W. Mbugua. 2020. Road Crash Trauma, Climate Change, Pollution and the Total Costs of Speed: Six Graphs that Tell the Story. GRSF Note 2020.1. Washington, DC: Global Road Safety Facility, World Bank.

Table 2: Assessment of Interventions for Managing Speed in CAREC Countries

Intervention Type	Road Safety Impact	Sustainability	Benefit–Cost Ratio	Safe System Contribution	Overall Recommended Priority for CAREC (and Most LMICs)
Road engineering that forces speed down (e.g. road humps, raised crossings, roundabouts)	High	High	Up to 17:1	Strong	Priority 1
Vehicle technology that forces speeds down (e.g. speed limiters, governing ISA)	High	High (needs enforcement to avoid tampering with the technology)	Up to 8:1	Strong	Priority 2
Behavior change via general deterrence (e.g. enforcement and campaigns based on enforcement and consequences) combined with low-speed limits	High	Weak	3:1 to 14:1	Weak	Priority 3
Road engineering that assists drivers to lower speeds (e.g., lower speed limits, reminder speed restriction signs, geometric design, traffic signals, stop signs)	Reasonably high	High	High, but not as high as road engineering that forces speeds down, and partly dependent on enforcement	Moderate	Priority 4 when used alone (however, it works better in combination with road engineering that forces speeds down and behavior change via general deterrence)
GLS with additional speed limits and higher penalties for speeding for novice drivers	Moderate	Moderate	Not known	Weak	Priority 5
Vehicle technology that assists drivers to lower speeds (e.g., advisory ISA)	Moderate	Moderate (can be turned off by the driver)	Much lower than speed governing technology	Moderate	Priority 6
Campaigns based on the risk of crashing	Weak	Weak	Low	Weak	Low priority (useful only if needed to gain more support for the introduction of stronger enforcement, and to show that these campaigns do not improve serious crash numbers so that enforcement can be implemented)
Education or driver training (in schools or driver skills)	Minimal to harmful	Weak	Zero	Zero	Low priority

CAREC = Central Asia Regional Economic Cooperation, GLS = graduated licensing scheme, ISA = intelligent speed adaptation, LMICs = low- and middle-income countries.
Note: Benefit–cost ratios available from LMICs are rare. See D.M. Bishai and A.A. Hyder. 2006. Modeling the Cost Effectiveness of Injury Interventions in Lower and Middle Income Countries: Opportunities and Challenges. *Cost Effectiveness and Resource Allocation*. 4. pp 1–11.
Source: Author.

Table 3: Speed Limits and Potential Savings of Fatalities in CAREC Countries

Country	Urban Speed Limit (km/h)	Comparison with Safe System Speed of 30 km/h (km/h)	Calculated Decrease in Deaths, Urban[a]	Rural Speed Limit (km/h)	Comparison with Safe System Speed of 70 km/h (km/h)[b]	Calculated Decrease in Deaths, Rural[a]
Afghanistan[c]	90	Too high by 60	17 times lower	90	Too high by 20	3 times lower
Azerbaijan	60	Too high by 30	6 times lower	90	Too high by 20	3 times lower
PRC	N/A	N/A	N/A	N/A	N/A	N/A
Georgia	60	Too high by 30	6 times lower	90	Too high by 20	3 times lower
Kazakhstan	60	Too high by 30	6 times lower	110	Too high by 40	6 times lower
Kyrgyz Republic	60	Too high by 30	6 times lower	90	Too high by 20	3 times lower
Mongolia	60	Too high by 30	6 times lower	80	Too high by 10	2 times lower
Pakistan	90	Too high by 60	17 times lower	110	Too high by 40	6 times lower
Tajikistan	60	Too high by 30	6 times lower	90	Too high by 20	3 times lower
Turkmenistan	60	Too high by 30	6 times lower	90	Too high by 20	3 times lower
Uzbekistan	70	Too high by 40	9 times lower	100	Too high by 30	4 times lower
Average for CAREC	67	Too high by 37		94	Too high by 24	
Average for countries with good road safety records[d]	53	Too high by 23		90	Too high by 20	

CAREC = Central Asia Regional Economic Cooperation, PRC = People's Republic of China, km/h = kilometers per hour.

[a] These are calculated by applying Nilsson's Power Model (G. Nilsson. 2004. *Traffic Safety Dimension and the Power Model to Describe the Effect of Speed on Safety*. Doctoral thesis. Lund, Sweden: Lund Institute of Technology). Six times lower means the number deaths would be divided by a factor of 6. These effects compare the current speed limit with achieving average speeds equal to safe system speeds. This is not purely a matter of changing the speed limits, but managing average speeds down to these levels with traffic calming and general deterrence.
[b] With improved road features, such as median separation and safe roadsides, speeds can safely be above 70 km/h.
[c] ADB placed its regular assistance to Afghanistan on hold effective 15 August 2021.
[d] The four global top performing countries are Netherlands, Norway, Sweden, and Switzerland; three of the best in the Asia and Pacific region are Singapore, Australia, and New Zealand.

Source: Analysis of data from World Health Organization. 2018. *Global Status Report on Road Safety*. Geneva.

As the data from the PRC suggest, lowering the speed limit by 10 km/h from 60 to 50km/h could reduce average speeds by 14 km/h (from 60 to 46 km/h).

As a guide to what can be achieved with speed management in the CAREC region, a reduction in average travel speeds of 10 km/h from the present limit would yield profound savings of death and disability. Just a 10 km/h reduction in average speeds would equal a 20% reduction in speed for a 50 km/h limit, 17% for a 60 km/h limit, 11% for a 90 km/h limit, and 10% for a 100 km/h limit. Applying the relationship from Nilsson's research[117]—that each 1% reduction in average speed results in a 4% reduction in deaths—reveals that these speed reductions would reduce road deaths in CAREC countries by 53%. No other direct change can achieve such an impressive saving of lives, or the economic benefits this will generate.

---

[117] G. Nilsson. 2004. *Traffic Safety Dimension and the Power Model to Describe the Effect of Speed on Safety*. Doctoral thesis. Lund, Sweden: Lund Institute of Technology.

The best use of proven interventions for each CAREC country will be influenced by the nature of the problems they in particular face. For example, if most speeding related serious crashes occur on rural and inter-urban roads, then targeting these may be the most critical step, but if the largest speed-related problem is that speed limits are too high, then lowering these along with increased interventions to improve compliance will be the step with the greatest potential benefits.

> *In CAREC countries, a 10 km/h reduction in average speeds in each of the most common speed limits would deliver a reduction in road deaths of approximately 53%. No other direct change can achieve such an impressive saving of lives, or the economic benefits this will generate.*

4: What can feasibly be achieved?

It is helpful to map decision-makers, potential partners, and other stakeholders for each intervention under consideration, and to assess feasibility based on the necessary partners and decision-makers. It will be helpful to engage them in decision-making for greater ownership. In speed management it is noteworthy that opposition can be vocal but still a minority of the community, and community surveys often show that most locally affected people want safe speeds on their roads.[118]

A further consideration in selecting suitable actions relates to political or other feasibility checks. This involves three factors: political feasibility, logistic feasibility, and having a willing partner organization (or your own organization) with the decision power and competency to achieve the implementation.

For example, the government may have made an election promise or other commitment not to implement a particular intervention, and so that intervention may not be politically feasible. Feasibility may also be challenged by logistic aspects of the road transport system, e.g., speed cameras are not feasible if a large proportion of vehicles are not registered or do not display a registration number for identification by the cameras. A guide can be used to assess a country's readiness for speed cameras.[119] For effective speed management, feasibility will commonly depend on stakeholders such as the authority or department that sets speed limits, the authority or department managing road engineering and maintenance for traffic calming, and police for enforcement.

5: Is funding available, including from different partners?

The first considerations here is to determine implementation costs and the available budget. Costs can also be refined based on how much of the intervention is to be implemented e.g., 5,000 km of road with traffic calming, versus 100 km.

If funding is insufficient, seek funding from elsewhere. This may mean preparing a business case for your organization (or your section of your organization) or government to receive the funding or preparing a case for another organization to commit part of its budget to implementing the selected intervention, e.g., getting police to increase enforcement.

Alternatively, funding can be procured through changes in policies and standards. For example, a policy could be created that the department responsible for roads must implement 30 km/h zones, with traffic calming around all schools and pedestrianized shopping areas.

It may be helpful to reconsider the interventions chosen, based on which partners are responsible for implementing them and how willing and capable they are to implement.

---

[118] FIA Foundation & AIP Foundation. 2022. *Road Safety Citizen Engagement Study in Vietnam*; and L. Mooren, R. Grzebieta, and S. Job. 2013. *Speed: The Biggest and Most Contested Road Killer*. In Proceedings of the Australasian College of Road Safety Conference. Adelaide. October.

[119] S. Job et al. 2020. *Guide for Determining Readiness for Speed Cameras and Other Automated Enforcement*. Geneva: Global Road Safety Facility and the Global Road Safety Partnership.

This sequence of decision processes may be used iteratively, starting again at the first step if previous opportunities have been eliminated by these processes. However, there is no value in choosing ineffective or weak interventions to implement, and these can result in great harm by giving government and stakeholders the false impression that the situation is being improved, which will delay opportunities for future effective interventions.

B. Managing and Delivering Implementation

Road safety management is a substantial arena for which guidance already exists and does not need to be reconsidered here.[120] However, a few points on planning and management for speed are relevant here. It is critical that speed management is a dedicated pillar of any road safety plan or strategy. Subsuming speed management into behavior change results in a singular focus on enforcement (and education) to manage speed, a misguided and unhelpful approach given the much stronger BRCs available from traffic calming interventions. Unfortunately, many road safety strategies and plans invite this error by including speed management under the safe road users (or behavior change) pillar or by covering speed in broad terms without a specific pillar. More effective speed management arises in strategies that include safe speed as a separate pillar of road safety action, facilitating a broad approach to the issue, including all the opportunities for speed management in one area of focus, and allowing for a team of people dedicated to coordinating and managing these processes.[121]

For the implementation of new interventions or substantial changes to existing policies or practices, forming a strong project and/or policy leadership team, with relevant partners represented at a high senior level, is also an important step for coordination, aligned messaging, ownership, and commitment.

Guidance is provided here on further key processes for delivering speed management.

Persuade Key Decision-Makers, Required Partners, and Stakeholders to Support and Fund Speed Management Actions

Because speed management is generally misunderstood, as well as underestimated in importance and in achievability, persuasion of key stakeholders, decision-makers and partners is likely to be critical to successful speed management in most countries. It is important to map relevant partners, decision-makers, and stakeholders and target them for meetings, discussions, and perhaps (depending on their roles and willingness to support) inclusion in leadership and delivery teams.

This may entail lobbying or preparing business cases and media speaking points for partners, decision-makers, politicians, and various other stakeholders to support certain interventions. Road safety nongovernment organizations (NGOs) can be especially important influencers in gaining support for effective interventions, and speed management is a greater focus for many NGOs now that the Global Alliance of Road Safety NGOs has launched an Accountability Toolkit, which prioritizes speed management interventions.[122]

Modules II to V provided evidence for the success of recommended interventions; this module shows BCRs for speed management interventions. Module VII provides core evidence for the need to manage speed, the economic benefits this generates, and provides arguments to counter many myths and misunderstandings of speed management. This information can be adopted to build the business case, media releases, or less formal communications within your organization and outside it in support of relevant interventions.

---

[120] See T. Bliss and J. Breen. 2013. Road Safety Management Capacity Reviews and Safe System Projects Guidelines. No. 84203, pp. 1–136. World Bank; and C. Sakashita. 2019. *Strategies to Tackle the Speed Issue for Road Safety in the Asia-Pacific Region.* Bangkok: UNESCAP.

[121] Examples of strategies including the dedicated speed pillar include Australia, Ireland, and Qatar. Australian Transport Council. 2011. *National Road Safety Strategy 2011–2020.* Canberra: ACT; Road Safety Authority (Ireland). 2013. *Road Safety Strategy 2013—2020*; and National Traffic Safety Committee (Qatar). 2012. *2012–2021 Qatar National Road Safety Strategy: Safe Road Users, Safe Vehicles Safe Roads, Safe Speeds.* Doha: National Traffic Safety Committee.

[122] Global Alliance of Road Safety NGOs. 2023. *Alliance Accountability Toolkit.*

Identify Potential Risks and Develop Mitigation Strategies

It is important to assess risks and identify strategies to mitigate them, e.g., if too few appropriate staff are available to manage implementation or ongoing operations, training may be a solution; in the case of speed cameras, maintenance and accuracy calibration processes may be technically challenging, and some countries have managed this by contracting camera suppliers and operators to operate the cameras to a set standard for a certain number of years.

Conduct Monitoring, Evaluation, and Continuous Improvement

For persuasion or funding purposes, it may be necessary to implement a pilot program to show that the proposed intervention improves safety. In such cases planning for sound monitoring and evaluation from the start of the program is necessary, so that the extent of road safety impact can be established and a business case developed for expansion or refinement of successful programs. Even for full-scale programs, monitoring and evaluation is needed to defend the program based on its road safety benefits. This will often require collection of baseline and post implementation data, which should be planned into the implementation processes and budget. It is critical that the right locations and targets are chosen, which means that the locations should have significant numbers of serious crashes from which reductions can be made. Monitoring of effects of speed management interventions is important for continuous improvement, e.g., through identification of the particular circumstances in which an intervention delivers stronger safety outcomes or weaker safety outcomes.

Note that the political convenience of lowering speed limits where travel speeds are already lower than the existing limit will yield little in safety benefits, as such speeds will offer little room for improvement in safety. Because the relationship between speed and crashes is well established, even where crash data are inadequate for evaluation, achieving reductions in travel speeds is clear evidence of road safety success, and likely reductions in deaths and injuries can be calculated from speed reductions.

VII. Evidence for the Role of Speed in Crashes: Dispelling Myths and Misinformation

A. The Contribution of Speed to Crashes and Their Severity

The role and importance of speed in serious crashes is often underestimated. Most of us know that speed is a major determinant of crash severity, but many assume that speed does not influence crash occurrence. The evidence shows that speed is a critical contributor to both crash occurrence and severity, which is why changes in speed have a more powerful effect on serious crash numbers than on property damage only crash numbers.

Crash Occurrence

There are many causal sequences by which speed contributes to the occurrence of crashes:[123]

- As speed increases, so too does the distance a vehicle travels in the time a driver and rider takes to see a problem ahead, judge what to do, and react, because the vehicle is traveling faster for that available time. Thus, the vehicle is closer to any problem situation even before the driver has judged the need to stop and moved to brake.
- From a higher speed, once the brakes are applied a vehicle takes longer to stop.
- When traveling at higher speed, a driver is less likely to see a hazard in a busy road environment, simply because they have less time to visually scan the environment on approach.
- Drivers are less inclined to stop and give way when they are traveling at higher speeds due to the increased braking and then acceleration afterwards required to return to their original speed. Research shows a clear systematic relationship between driver approach speed and failing to yield to pedestrians at legal pedestrian crossings: at 32 km/h around 75% of drivers yield to pedestrians, but at just 16 km/h higher speed, only 40% of drivers yield to pedestrians (Figure 5).[124]
- At night, even moderate speed in a poorly lit urban environment can mean a vehicle is traveling at a speed that results in a combined judgement, reaction time, and stopping distance that make it impossible to stop within the distance illuminated by the headlights. Thus, a crash with a pedestrian or hazard on the road may be unavoidable by the time it is visible.[125] The distance along the road made visible by headlights (even on high beam) can also be less that the combined judgement, reaction time, and stopping distance on rural roads with high travel speeds.
- At higher speed a driver is less able to maneuver and stay in control of their vehicle to get around a problem and avoid a crash.
- At higher speed a vehicle is less able to negotiate a curve or corner without losing control and running off the road or crossing to the wrong side of the road, risking a head-on crash. This is not a rare form of head-on crash on rural roads, with studies showing that curves are associated with more head-on crashes,[126] and that head-on crashes are mostly not caused by overtaking, but rather driving at too-high speeds.[127]

---

[123] R. F. S. Job and C. Brodie. 2022. Understanding the Role of Speeding and Speed in Serious Crash Trauma: A Case Study of New Zealand. *Journal of Road Safety.* 33 (1). pp. 5–25; and R. F. S. Job and S. Sakashita. 2016. Management of Speed: The Low-Cost, Rapidly Implementable Effective Road Safety Action to Deliver the 2020 Road Safety Targets. *Journal of the Australasian College of Road Safety.* May. pp. 65–70.

[124] T. Bertulis and D. M. Dulaski. 2014. Driver Approach Speed and Its Impact on Driver Yielding to Pedestrian Behavior at Unsignalized Crosswalks. *Transportation Research Record.* 2464 (1). pp. 46–51.

[125] R. H. Grzebieta. 2019. *Safe Speed Limits.* Prepared for Trauma Week 2019 Symposium, Pedestrians – Staying Safe. Royal Australasian College Surgeons. Melbourne,.13 February.

[126] M. Hosseinpour, A. S. Yahaya, and A. F. Sadullah. 2014. Exploring the Effects of Roadway Characteristics on the Frequency and Severity of Head-On Crashes: Case Studies from Malaysian Federal Roads. *Accident Analysis & Prevention.* 62. pp. 209–222.

[127] P. Gårder. 2006. Segment Characteristics and Severity of Head-On Crashes on Two-Lane Rural Highways in Maine. *Accident Analysis & Prevention.* 38 (4). pp. 652–661.

- Based on the topography of the road, higher speeds reduce the time from when a risk becomes visible to a driver to when evasive action is required. For example, a low speed may be required because of curves limiting vision for intersections or junctions just beyond the curve, and thus the speed limit is set to allow enough time for entering or crossing vehicles (or pedestrians) to do so safely in the time they have before a vehicle which is just out of view behind the curve would reach them, and enough time for a vehicle traveling along the road with the curve to see, judge, and stop. However, a speeding vehicle can reach the intersection too quickly, causing a crash. The same logic applies to other road features such as crests of hills, which limit vision ahead.
- Even if in view, other road users (especially pedestrians) may reasonably expect an approaching vehicle to take a certain time to reach them at the prevailing speed limit allowing them time to cross, yet a speeding vehicle may reach them sooner than expected. This is especially true for older pedestrians who tend to judge a safe crossing gap by the distance to the approaching vehicle more than the speed of the vehicle.[128]

Crash Severity

There are also multiple causal sequences by which speed contributes to crash severity, as described in the following.

- The higher the speed, the higher the energy and more deadly the forces in a crash. Speed is the toxin in crashes, with higher speeds delivering exponentially more energy into the crash.[129] Speed has especially powerful and exponential effects on crash severity because the kinetic energy of a vehicle is not just proportional to its speed but to the square of its speed. For example, when impact speed increases from 30 km/h to 50 km/h (a 67% increase in speed), the energy increases by 178%.

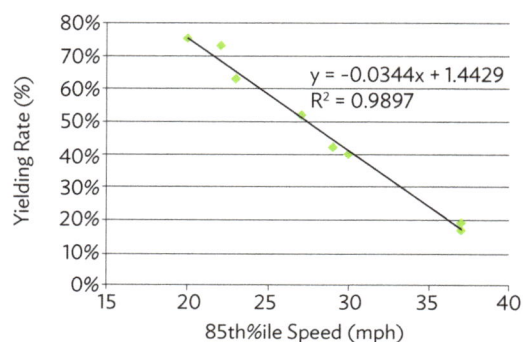

Figure 5: Relationship Between the Rate of Drivers Yielding to Pedestrians and Approach Speed

mph = miles per hour
Note:
In this study, approach speed is measured as the 85th percentile, which is the speed exceeded by 15% of vehicles.
Source: T. Bertulis and D.M. Dulaski. Driver Approach Speed and Its Impact on Driver Yielding to Pedestrian Behavior at Unsignalized Crosswalks. *Transportation Research Record*. 2464 (1). pp. 46–51

- Safety features of the road, such as crash barriers, are located, designed, and built to provide protection up to the speed limit, but may become ineffective if hit at speeds above the limit.[130] Thus, as speed increases safety features of the road designed to manage crash forces and/or prevent the vehicle from a more severe crash are less able to perform their safety function effectively. It is no simple matter to build all barriers, medians, etc. to withstand high speeds: The high construction costs limit other road safety work and may not be possible with the space available on many roads.
- As speed increases, active vehicle safety features such as automatous emergency braking are less able to be activated in time to avoid a crash, or less able to reduce speed to safe levels of impact by the time the crash impact occurs.

---

[128] R.F.S. Job et al. 1998. *Pedestrians at Traffic Light Controlled Intersections: Crossing Behavior in the Elderly and Non-Elderly*. In K. Smith, B.G. Aitken, and R.H. Grzebieta, eds. Proceedings of the Conference on Pedestrian Safety. pp. 3–11. Canberra: Australian College of Road Safety & Federal Office of Road Safety.

[129] R. F. S. Job and C. Brodie. 2022. Understanding the Role of Speeding and Speed in Serious Crash Trauma: A Case Study of New Zealand. *Journal of Road Safety*. 33 (1). pp. 5–25.; and Insurance Institute for Highway Safety. Speed.

[130] New Zealand Transport Agency Waka Kotahi. 2021. Specification & Guidelines for Road Safety Hardware & Devices. Wellington: Waka Kotahi NZ Transport Agency.

- As speed increases, the passive protective features of vehicles become less effective: the integrity of the vehicle body may fail, crushing the occupants and leaving little survival room; restraint systems (i.e., airbags, seat belts) may be unable to minimize higher levels of force sufficiently to avoid severe injury or death.

These contributions, on top of direct contributions to crashes occurring at all, are the reason why extensive analyses of scientific studies from many countries find that as speeds increase, fatal crashes show the largest percentage increase in occurrence, followed by injury crashes, followed by non-injury crashes.

B. The Contributions of Speed to Crash Trauma

Higher speeds contribute dramatically to serious crash risk through the processes listed above. This section presents the evidence showing how critical speed is for road safety. This evidence can be grouped into four areas of research, each with profound practical implications:[131]

1. The effects of changes in travel speed on serious crash risk.
2. Case-control studies of speed and serious crash risk.
3. The effects of impact speed on the chances of surviving the crash.
4. The evidence for life and injury-saving effects from many interventions that reduce speeds.

The Effects of Changes in Travel Speed on Serious Crash Risk

The effects of changes in travel speed (e.g., traffic calming road designs, enforcement) have been evaluated in hundreds of studies across many countries. These studies were assessed for their scientific rigor and valid studies were combined in a synthesis to determine the real effects of changes in speed on deaths, injuries, and crashes (Figure 6). Subsequent re-analyses and follow-up research evaluations validate these fundamental influences of speed on safety, and even suggest that this graph may slightly underestimate the importance of speed.[132] This evidence demonstrates that changes in speed have even greater impacts on higher severity crash outcomes with very small changes in speed having dramatic impacts on fatal outcomes.

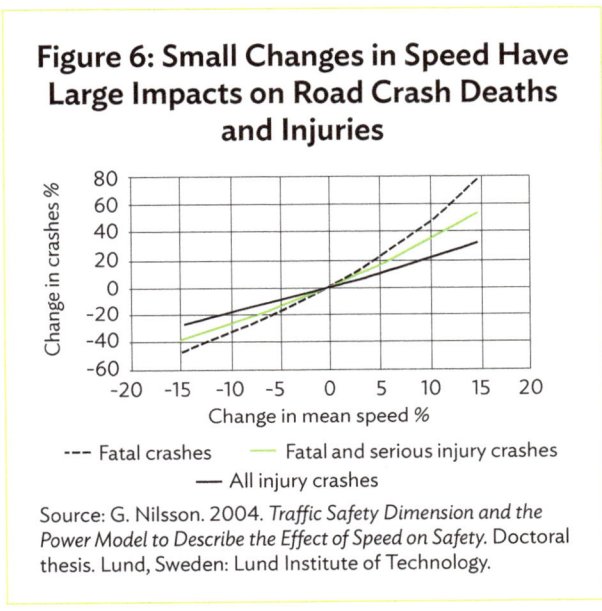

Figure 6: Small Changes in Speed Have Large Impacts on Road Crash Deaths and Injuries

--- Fatal crashes
— Fatal and serious injury crashes
— All injury crashes

Source: G. Nilsson. 2004. *Traffic Safety Dimension and the Power Model to Describe the Effect of Speed on Safety.* Doctoral thesis. Lund, Sweden: Lund Institute of Technology.

As a practical example, these results show that changes that produce a 10% reduction in average travel speed will deliver around a 40% reduction in deaths and around a 30% reduction in serious injuries.[133]

---

[131] Some of these brief sections are in part based on R.F.S. Job and L.W. Mbugua. 2020. *Road Crash Trauma, Climate Change, Pollution and the Total Costs of Speed: Six Graphs that Tell the Story.* GRSF Note 2020.1. Washington, DC: World Bank.

[132] R. Elvik et al. 2009. *The Handbook of Road Safety Measures.* Bingley, UK: Emerald Group Publishing Limited; R. Elvik. 2010. A Restatement of the Case for Speed Limits. *Transport Policy.* 17 (3). pp. 196–204; R. Elvik. 2013. A Re-parameterisation of the Power Model of the Relationship Between the Speed of Traffic and the Number of Accidents and Accident Victims. *Accident Analysis & Prevention.* 50. pp. 854–60; and R. Elvik et al. 2019. Updated Estimates of the Relationship Between Speed and Road Safety at the Aggregate and Individual Levels. *Accident Analysis & Prevention.* 123. pp. 114–122.

[133] The curve gradually changes slope as large changes in speed occur.

The applicability of the relationship in Figure 5 to LMICs including CAREC countries is clearly supported by research in LMICs:

» Analysis in Shanghai, PRC, showed a clear relationship between speeds and crash risk.[134]
» A study of factors in crash severity on motorways in Pakistan identified speed as a critical factor.[135]
» A study of the effects of speed interventions in Bangladesh showed substantial safety gains from lower speeds and a similar relationship to the power relationship observed in HICs.[136]
» Further examples of safety successes from lowering speeds in CAREC and other LMICs are provided in relation to specific interventions elsewhere in this manual.

Case-Control Studies of Speed and Serious Crash Risk

Instead of examining the effects of changes in speed (due to various interventions), another scientific method for determining the effects of speed on crash risk is to examine the speeds of drivers who are involved in crashes and compare these with the speeds of other drivers (controls) who are driving past the location of the crash at the same time of day as the crash occurred. Several such studies exist, allowing assessment of the risks of the speed of individual vehicles traveling along the same road, at the same location, and at the same time of day.

These studies again reveal the powerful effects of speed on serious crash risk. For example, an Australian study found that for 60 km/h speed limits, each 5 km/h above the speed limit resulted in a doubling of the risk of a casualty (fatal or injury) crash.[137] Similarly, another study in Victoria, Australia over multiple speed zones found that at 5 km/h over the limit, injury crash risk was 44% higher, and at 10 km/h over the limit, the risk was 108% higher.[138] Other studies reveal similarly powerful effects of chosen travel speed on serious crash risk,[139] though the doubling of risk occurs at slightly larger increases in speed in higher speed limit zones,[140] consistent with the earlier reported finding that the percentage change in speed determines serious crash risk.

The Effects of Impact Speed on the Chances of Surviving the Crash

Another method for determining the importance of speed in serious crash risk is to assess crash impact speeds and the chance of a death at that speed. This is done separately for different crash types (pedestrians, car side impact, head-on crash, etc.) because the ability of the vehicle to protect people changes with the crash type. Figure 7 shows a simplified summary of the risk of deaths for each impact speed for different crash types: pedestrian crashes, crashes into rigid objects, side impact crashes, and head-on crashes. As shown, the influence of speed on risk of death is profound, and is the basis of the safe system speed limits.[141]

---

[134] X. Wang et al. 2018. Speed, Speed Variation and Crash Relationships for Urban Arterials. *Accident Analysis & Prevention*. 113. pp. 236–243.
[135] N. Ahmad et al. 2022. Exploring Factors Associated with Crash Severity on Motorways in Pakistan. *Proceedings of the Institution of Civil Engineers–Transport*. 175 (4). pp. 189–198.
[136] A. R. van der Horst et al. 2017. An Evaluation of Speed Management Measures in Bangladesh Based Upon Alternative Accident Recording, Speed Measurements, and DOCTOR Traffic Conflict Observations. *Transportation Research Part F: Traffic Psychology and Behavior*. 46. pp. 390–403.
[137] C. N. Kloeden, J. McLean, and G. F. V. Glonek. 2002. *Reanalysis of Travelling Speed and the Risk of Crash Involvement in Adelaide, South Australia*. Canberra: Australian Transport Safety Bureau.
[138] M. Fitzharris et al. 2020. *Enhanced Crash Investigation Study–Report 1; Overview and Analysis of Crash Types, Injury Outcomes and Contributing Factors*. Clayton, Australia: Monash University.
[139] T. Brenac et al. 2015. Influence of Travelling Speed on the Risk of Injury Accident: a Matched Case-Control Study. *Periodica Polytechnica Transportation Engineering*. 43 (3). pp. 129–137.
[140] C. N. Kloeden and A. J. McLean. 2001. *Rural Speed and Crash Risk*. In Proceedings of the Australasian Road Safety Research, Policing and Education Conference. 5. Monash University.
[141] Global Road Safety Partnership. 2008. *Speed Management: A Road Safety Manual for Decision-Makers and Practitioners*. Geneva.

More recent rigorous syntheses and studies show slightly higher speeds for the risk of pedestrian death[142] and lower impact speeds for the risk of serious injury rather than death,[143] with the shapes of the curves remaining similar.

Evidence for Life- and Injury-Saving Effects from Speed Reduction Interventions

Many hundreds of scientific studies have found that the various interventions that reduce speeds also powerfully reduce crash deaths and injuries. The first type of study presented above, of the effects of changes in travel speed, is based on synthesis of the results of individual studies of the safety benefits of lower speeds, achieved in various ways. The evidence on many effective interventions extends to demonstrating excellent BCRs, as presented later.

Examples of such successful savings of life and injury through lowering speeds are presented here to (i) highlight the irrefutable evidence of the value of lower speeds, and (ii) identify key intervention opportunities for saving lives and injuries through lowering speeds in CAREC countries.

These examples are divided into three broad areas of intervention:

1. **Traffic calming.** Road engineering interventions.
2. **Enforcement and promotion.** Behavior change interventions.
3. **Vehicle technology.** Vehicle interventions to help limit speeds.

The intervention types were presented in detail, along with the evidence for their effectiveness, with a module devoted to each.

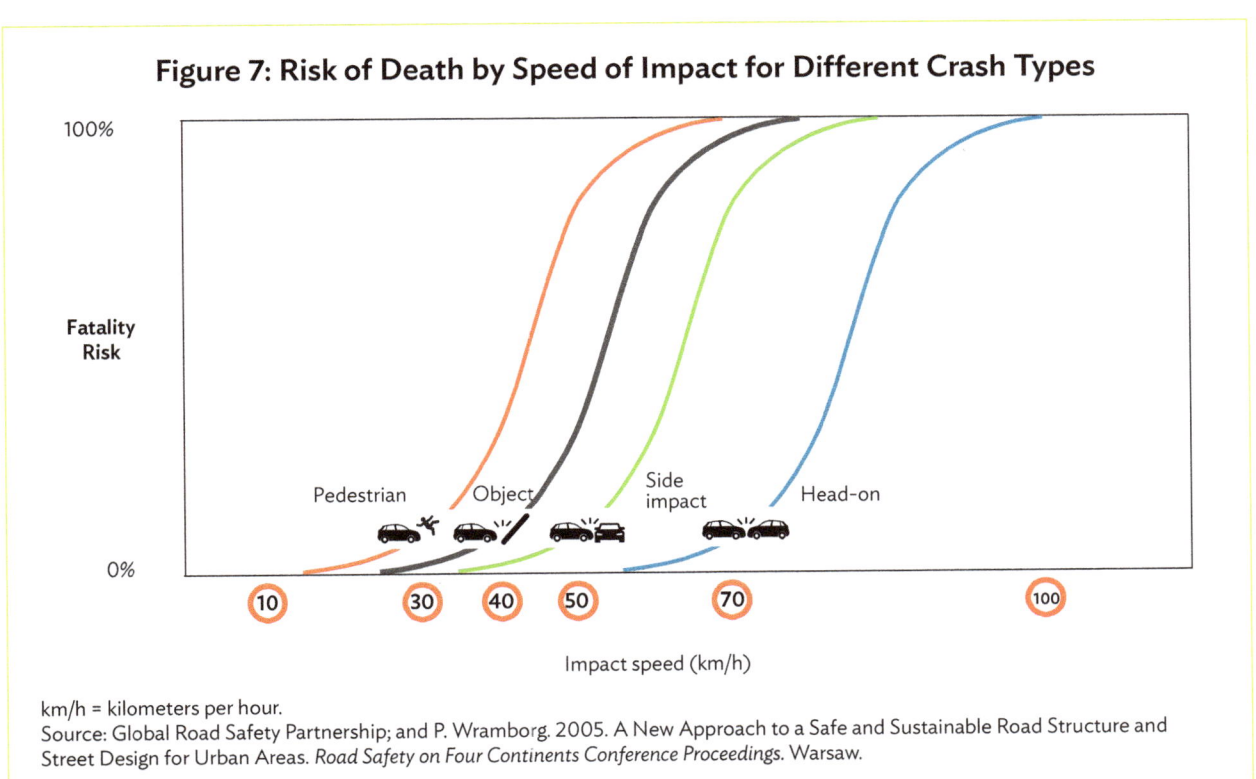

km/h = kilometers per hour.
Source: Global Road Safety Partnership; and P. Wramborg. 2005. A New Approach to a Safe and Sustainable Road Structure and Street Design for Urban Areas. *Road Safety on Four Continents Conference Proceedings.* Warsaw.

---

[142] Q. Hussain et al. 2019. The Relationship Between Impact Speed and the Probability of Pedestrian Fatality during a Vehicle–Pedestrian Crash: A Systematic Review and Meta-Analysis. *Accident Analysis & Prevention.* 129. pp. 241–249.

[143] S. D. Doecke et al. 2021. Travel Speed and the Risk of Serious Injury in Vehicle Crashes. *Accident Analysis & Prevention.* 161. 106359; and C. Jurewicz et al. 2016. Exploration of Vehicle Impact Speed–Injury Severity Relationships for Application in Safer Road Design. *Transportation Research Procedia.* 14. pp. 4247–4256.

C. Economic Costs of Crash Deaths and Injuries

All these benefits of lower speeds not only improve human life quality and longevity, but also reduce the real costs of transport to a nation.

One of the least understood areas of cost of crashes is the cost of losing people from the workforce, either permanently, through death or disability, or temporarily due to serious injury from which the person eventually recovers. In addition to health system costs, deaths and disabilities remove productive people from the workforce and often also remove another family member from productive work to care for the victim. In many cases, a lifetime of productivity is lost. Road crash deaths and disabilities are especially costly to a society because of the typical age of death or injury, with the age group from 18 to 25 years old being most as risk of death globally. Most crash deaths take people who are in economically productive age groups, including in CAREC countries, where on average over 80% of people killed in crashes are in productive age groups (Table 4). By comparison, the most common causes of death (heart failure, stroke, and cancer) typically kill people who are around retirement age or older. While all deaths are individual human tragedies, the older deaths generate dramatically less economic cost.

Table 4 also shows estimates of the economic costs of road crash deaths and injuries based on best existing economic methodologies. These costs, expressed as a percentage of gross domestic product (GDP) lost each year, are a significant proportion of GDP each year for every CAREC country. The cost of crash deaths and injuries averages 4.7% of GDP in the LMICs of the Asia and Pacific region each year,[144] compared with an average of 5.0% in CAREC countries in the same year,[145] meaning that crashes on average cost more economically in CAREC countries than in the Asia and Pacific region overall. The latest estimate for CAREC countries is a cost of 4.6% of GDP per year. These data show a full appreciation of the huge economic costs of road crashes in each CAREC country and highlight the pure economic value of improving road safety, on top of the human suffering, loss, and grief.

Currently, in effect, many of the real costs of road transport are hidden because they are not seen as due to transport and not measured as such, so the economic savings of safe speeds are also missed. Thus, managing speed is one of the most cost-effective ways to reduce serious crashes and their economic costs.

Several studies have combined multiple costs and benefits of speed to assess economically ideal speeds on different road types. The reliable finding is that the economically ideal speed is substantially lower than current speeds and speed limits. Figure 8 shows the economic costs of travel at various speeds on a divided carriageway (motorway, not highway or rural road) in Iran. This study found that the economically ideal speed for the motorway for society overall was 73 km/h, well below the speed limits applied globally to motorways, which are often 100 km/h to 120 km/h.

Other studies report similar results, with the supposed economic value of higher speed consistently found not to exist. In Spain, a study found that a reduction of speed limits on highways and freeways would benefit the economy and that the optimum speed limit was around 70 km/h.[146] In Australia, on 100 km/h speed-limited sealed rural roads with 3.5 m wide lanes, the economically ideal speed was around 85 km/h for trucks and between 85 km/h and 90 km/h for cars, depending on the extent of curves.[147]

Meanwhile in LMICs, a study in Türkiye on the effects of a proposed speed increase from 90 km/h to 100 km/h found the economic costs would outweigh the economic benefits.[148] A study in the notoriously congested city of Sao Paulo, Brazil, assessed the

---

[144] World Bank. 2019. *Guide for Road Safety Opportunities and Challenges: Low- and Middle-Income Countries Country Profiles.* Washington, DC.

[145] W. Wambulwa and R. F. S. Job. 2019. *Guide for Road Safety Opportunities and Challenges: Low- and Middle-Income Countries Country Profiles.* Washington, DC: World Bank. Calculation methods are based on K. McMahon and S. Dahdah. 2008. *The True Cost of Road Crashes, Valuing Life and the Cost of a Serious Injury.* International Road Assessment Programme.

[146] V. A. de Albornoz. 2022. Road Speed Limit Matters–Are Politicians Doing the Right Thing? *Socio-Economic Planning Sciences.* 79. 101106.

[147] M. Cameron. 2003. *Potential Benefits and Costs of Speed Changes on Rural Roads.* Report CR216. Victoria, Australia: Monash University Accident Research Centre; and M. Cameron. 2012. Optimum Speeds on Rural Roads Based on 'Willingness to Pay' Values of Road Trauma. *Journal of the Australasian College of Road Safety.* 23 (3):67–74.

[148] V. R. Cetin, H. H. Yilmaz, and V. Erkan. 2018. The Impact of Increasing Speed Limit in Turkey: The Case of Ankara-Sivrihisar Road Section. *Case Studies on Transport Policy.* 6 (1). pp. 72–80.

Table 4: Cost of Crashes Each Year in CAREC Countries
(%)

Country	Afghanistan	Azerbaijan	PRC	Georgia	Kazakhstan	Kyrgyz Republic	Mongolia	Pakistan	Tajikistan	Turkmenistan	Uzbekistan	AVERAGE (unweighted)
Income Classification	Low	Upper-Middle	Upper-Middle	Upper-Middle	Upper-Middle	Lower-Middle	Lower-Middle	Lower-Middle	Lower-Middle	Upper-Middle	Lower-Middle	–
% of deaths in economically productive age group (15–64 years)	80	80	72	79	82	84	84	75	82	86	84	80.7
Cost of crash deaths and injuries as % of GDP per year (2016 deaths data)	5.0	2.9	6.2	5.3	5.9	5.0	5.5	4.7	6.0	4.8	3.8	5.0
Cost of crash deaths and injuries as % of GDP per year (updated with 2019 data)	5.3	2.2	5.9	4.4	4.2	4.2	7.0	4.3	5.2	4.5	3.8	4.6[a]

CAREC = Central Asia Regional Economic Cooperation, GDP = gross domestic product, PRC = People's Republic of China.
[a] Crash costs as a percentage of GDP each year decreased slightly from 2016 to 2019 in CAREC. However, in most CAREC countries this is mainly due to an increase in GDP across those years, rather than an improvement in road safety.
Notes:
The cut off for lower-middle to upper middle income is $4,255 gross national income per capita.
For income classification details, see World Bank. 2022. World Bank Country and Lending Groups.
Sources: W. Wambulwa & R. F. S. Job. 2019. *Guide for Road Safety Opportunities and Challenges: Low- and Middle-Income Countries.* Washington, DC. World Bank, 2022, and World Health Organization 2019 update.

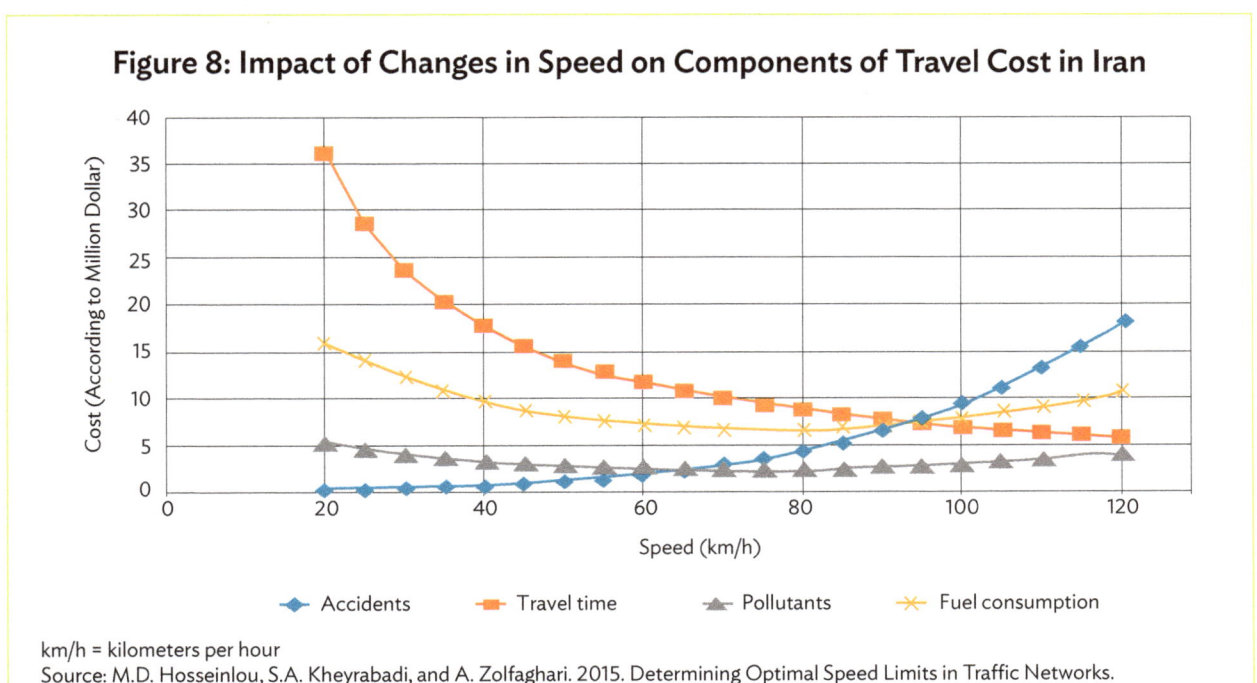

Figure 8: Impact of Changes in Speed on Components of Travel Cost in Iran

km/h = kilometers per hour
Source: M.D. Hosseinlou, S.A. Kheyrabadi, and A. Zolfaghari. 2015. Determining Optimal Speed Limits in Traffic Networks. *International Association of Traffic and Safety Sciences.* 39 (1). pp. 36–41.

economic impacts of lower speed limits and found that the economic saving from reduced crashes, deaths, and injuries alone outweighed the economic cost of slightly longer journey times, even with existing congestion.[149] Furthermore, these studies and others have not considered all costs (e.g., the above studies do not include health costs of air pollution or noise exposure costs).[150] Thus, they overestimate the economically ideal speed, which may be lower when full costs are included.

Retarded Long-Term Economic Growth

Crashes cause substantial economic costs for countries as described above, causing retarded long-term GDP growth. A detailed economic analysis of five LMICs in Asia and Africa showed that halving deaths and injuries (i.e., meeting the UN target for 2030) will increase GDP per capita over 24 years by between 7.1% and 22.2%.[151] All countries will benefit from improved long-term economic growth by reducing crash deaths and injuries, some by almost 1% each year for 24 years.[152]

Calculation of the Effects of Crash Trauma on Long-Term Economic Growth in the CAREC Region

A detailed assessment of the economic effects of crash trauma (deaths and injuries) was undertaken for four CAREC countries: Kazakhstan, the Kyrgyz Republic, Tajikistan, and Uzbekistan.[153] Retarded long-term economic growth was calculated by considering the increased growth that would be achieved only through the impacts of a single but maintained 10% reduction in human days lost due to injury or death among the working age population. Even with this narrow consideration of costs and this much more modest reduction (10%, not 50% as used in the study of four countries mentioned), the effects in the CAREC region are profound. The results show that a 10% reduction in crash trauma would save human costs by an amount equivalent to a significant proportion of the 2019 GDP of these countries, ranging from 2.7% in Tajikistan to 6.4% in Kazakhstan.

The effects of road crash trauma on overall economic development of these CAREC countries are also substantial. The same hypothetical 10% reduction would significantly enhance economic growth: by 2048 per capita GDP would be significantly higher in each country, ranging up to an extra 5.5% of 2019 GDP in the Kyrgyz Republic. These changes from a modest 10% reduction in (some, not all) relevant crash costs highlight the retarding effects of crashes on economic growth currently being suffered in CAREC. Achieving the UN target for the current Decade of Road Safety, a 50% reduction in deaths and injuries, would deliver dramatically larger improvements in long-term economic growth in CAREC.

The Importance of Speed Data and the Use of Crash Data to Estimate the Role of Speed and Speeding

One cause of the under-appreciation of the role of speed in causing crashes and making them more severe arises from how speeding is recorded in crash data in most countries. Typically, crash data include the number of crashes that are reported to involve speeding, which comes primarily from police reports of crashes. These data vary from country to country, with the estimates generally ranging from 25% to 40% of fatal crashes involving speeding, including in CAREC countries.[154] However, discussions with police officers in various countries reveal that they believe that speeding is a much larger factor than their

---

[149] A. Ang, P. Christensen, and R. Vieira. 2020. Should Congested Cities Reduce Their Speed Limits? Evidence from São Paulo, Brazil. *Journal of Public Economics.* (184). 104155.

[150] R. F. S. Job, and S. Sakashita. 2016. Management of Speed: The Low-Cost, Rapidly Implementable Effective Road Safety Action to Deliver the 2020 Road Safety Targets. *Journal of the Australasian College of Road Safety.* May. pp. 65–70; and WHO. 2011. *Burden of Disease from Environmental Noise: Quantification of Healthy Life Years Lost in Europe.* WHO Regional Office for Europe.

[151] World Bank. 2017. *The High Toll of Traffic Injuries: Unacceptable and Preventable.* Advisory Services and Analytics Technical Report P155310. Washington, DC.

[152] D. Bose, P. Marquez , S. Job. 2018. The Economic Growth and Welfare Impacts of Reducing Road Crash Deaths and Injuries. *Connections Note.* Washington, DC: World Bank.

[153] World Bank. 2022. *Socioeconomic Impacts of Road Traffic Injuries in Central Asia.* Washington, DC.

[154] E.g., 38% in Kazakhstan, in K. Ibrayev et al. 2019. Analysis of the State of the Road Traffic Safety in the Republic of Kazakhstan. Наука и техника. (6). pp. 482–489; and for Pakistan see N. Ahmad et al. 2022. Exploring factors associated with crash severity on motorways in Pakistan. In *Proceedings of the Institution of Civil Engineers-Transport.* 175 (4). pp. 189–198).

data indicate, sometimes suggesting that speeding is involved in 50% or even 80% of fatal crashes.[155] In the many crashes where police cannot determine whether speeding was involved, it is not included as a factor. Similarly, members of the Mongolian National Road Safety Council and the country's Traffic Police Department agree that speeding is underestimated as a factor in fatal and serious crashes. For example, at the scene of a pedestrian fatality, the driver may be the only person who can report what happened. That driver is most unlikely to admit to speeding and may blame the pedestrian by claiming they rushed out and the driver did not have time to stop. Unless there are skid marks or witnesses, determining whether the crash involved speeding is difficult. Similarly, speeding is difficult to identify in single vehicle run-off road crashes and many other crashes.

There is, however, a scientific way to adjust for the likely number of missed speeding-involved fatal crashes. Studies have compared police reports of speeding involvement in particular crashes with better evidence to determine the real involvement of speeding, and comparing this with crash data indicates that speeding is involved in around twice as many fatal crashes as the data indicate. This can be used as a correction factor, by doubling the estimated number in crash data. The better evidence comes from in-depth crash investigations, crash reconstructions, and modern vehicle event recorder systems (the equivalent of a flight recorder "black box"), which reveal the speeds involved in crashes much more accurately. If this correction factor is applied to crash data, it approximately doubles the number of fatal crashes involving speeding. This type of analysis for New Zealand showed that from crash data indicating that over 29% of fatal crashes involved speeding, the best estimate for the real number is 60% (footnote 160). Note that some crashes were reported with multiple causes.

Applying this evidence-based correction factor indicates that well over half the fatal and serious crashes in CAREC countries involve speeding. As explained later in this module, on average crashes cost CAREC countries 4.6% of GDP, which indicates that speeding-related crashes are on average costing CAREC countries over 2.3% of GDP each year. This is an avoidable economic drain on CAREC countries. Speed-related but non-speeding crashes, which occur where speed limits are too high for safety, add to this burden.

Speed data are in themselves a vital tool for road safety and the management of speed. These allow for evaluations and refinements to speed management interventions. In the absence of valid comprehensive crash data knowing the changes in speed generated by interventions (and applying the speed-risk relationships) also allows for sound prediction of the changes in deaths, injuries, and changes these will produce. Thus, on-road (not self-reported) surveys of travel are vitally important data for road safety management.

Speeding-related crashes cost CAREC countries over 2.3% of GDP on average each year—an avoidable economic drain for these countries.

D. The Known Effects of Speed Apply in CAREC Countries

The effects of speed on crashes are determined by the laws of physics applied to the details of the transport system, and thus there is no reason to expect that the risks and costs of speed do not apply in CAREC countries. Indeed, information from CAREC countries directly supports this and identifies that speed is even more critical to safety and other costs of road transport than in HICs. This is apparent from various elements of the road transport system across CAREC countries compared with best practice, as described in Table 5. Descriptions are general across CAREC, with features generally applying but not all applying equally in all CAREC countries.

---

[155] R. F. S. Job & C. Brodie. 2022. Understanding the Role of Speeding and Speed in Serious Crash Trauma: A Case Study of New Zealand. *Journal of Road Safety*. 33 (1). pp. 5–25.; and S. Job et al. 2015. *Federative Republic of Brazil: National Road Safety Management Capacity Review*. Report No: AUS13128. November; Washington, DC: Global Road Safety Facility, World Bank.

Table 5: Features of CAREC Countries That Demonstrate the Importance of Speed Reduction

System Factor	Features in Common Across CAREC Countries that Make Speed Critical	Features in CAREC Countries That Make Speed More Critical than in Good Performing Road Safety Countries	Consequences for Speed Management
Roads	Basic features of roads in CAREC countries include roads with painted center lines rather than median barriers, urban roads with unprotected pedestrian access, and unprotected use by other VRUs.	CAREC countries have a high proportion of unsealed or "dirt" roads.	Unsealed roads are less forgiving of even small human errors, and so lower speeds are needed.
Roadsides	Many roads have roadsides involving steep drops or are lined by unforgiving objects if hit in a crash.	CAREC countries overall have higher risk non-urban roadsides (i.e., more mountainous roads with steep roadside drops, more curves and blind spots), and tend to have fewer safety barriers to protect road users.	High-risk roadsides on mountainous roads deserve lower speed limits to minimize risk (or extensive use of crash barriers to protect road users from human error).
		In some CAREC countries, on open plains/steppes roads are built up to manage snow and water, which results in unforgiving drops on both sides of the road.	High-risk roadsides, such as those with roadside drops of more than 2 meters, deserve lower speed limits.
		CAREC countries overall have some features that add to serious crash risk in urban areas, e.g., fewer available footpaths due to shops, parking, and other activities taking over the footpath, forcing pedestrians to walk on the streets.	More crashes will involve pedestrians, and thus on average even moderate speed creates much greater risk of death.
Vehicles	Vehicles do not protect occupants effectively in higher speed crashes.	CAREC countries overall enforce fewer of the relevant UN vehicle safety regulations.[a] Some CAREC countries (PRC, Mongolia, and Pakistan) have higher proportions of motorcycles, while some CAREC countries (such as Georgia and Mongolia) have a significant mix of left and right drive vehicles.	Safe system speeds protect road users, and should over time become the basis of speed management.
Road Users	CAREC countries have the same human risk of error, overconfidence, and vulnerability of the human body to physical force in a crash.	No profound differences.	All countries will benefit from lower speed limits.
Vulnerable Road Users (pedestrians, cyclists, motorcyclists)	In all countries, VRUs are at greater risk due to not having the protection of being inside a vehicle. Pedestrians are the most killed overall of the VRUs, including for CAREC countries, though in some countries it can be motorcycle occupants.	In CAREC countries overall, a higher proportion of deaths are pedestrians. Table 6 shows the relevant data on pedestrians deaths (selected because WHO does not provide data on motorcycle deaths in the CAREC countries with the highest rates of motorcycle use, making this difficult to assess)	Pedestrians are a larger issue in CAREC countries and require lower speeds for protection because of their vulnerability (lack of protection by a vehicle).

continued on next page

Table 5 continued

System Factor	Features in Common Across CAREC Countries that Make Speed Critical	Features in CAREC Countries That Make Speed More Critical than in Good Performing Road Safety Countries	Consequences for Speed Management
Speed limits	All countries have speed limits and most (including in CAREC) adhere to global guidelines on speed limit signage.	Default speed limits are often higher in CAREC countries. As a guide to the importance of speed limits for safety, it is also noteworthy that the generally lower speed limits are associated with higher incomes per capita.	Speed is more critical for deaths and injuries in CAREC countries than in good performing road safety countries, yet speed limits are higher. Lower default urban and rural speed limits in CAREC will dramatically reduce deaths and injuries. If default urban and rural speed limits were reduced to the average for the strong road safety countries then urban road deaths would be dramatically reduced. Lower speed limits will also improve the economies of CAREC countries.

CAREC = Central Asia Regional Economic Cooperation, PRC = People's Republic of China, UN = United Nations, VRUs = vulnerable road users, WHO = World Health Organization.

[a] Wambulwa W. & Job RFS. 2019. *Guide for Road Safety Opportunities and Challenges: Low- and Middle-Income Countries Country Profiles.* Washington, DC.;: World Bank.

Source: Author.

Table 6: Pedestrians in Crash Deaths in CAREC Countries

Country	Afghanistan	Azerbaijan	PRC	Georgia	Kazakhstan	Kyrgyz Republic	Mongolia	Pakistan	Tajikistan	Turkmenistan	Uzbekistan	Average for CAREC	Average For Good Road Safety Countries
% of deaths that are pedestrians	No data	42%	No data	27%	31%	40%	29%	No data	40%	No data	No data	33.8%	16.4%

CAREC = Central Asia Regional Economic Cooperation.
Note: These are four global top performing countries: Sweden, Netherlands, Norway, and Switzerland; and three of the best in the Asia and the Pacific region: Singapore, Australia, and New Zealand.
Source: Analysis of data from World Health Organization. 2018. *Global Status Report on Road Safety*. Geneva; and reports by countries.

Features of CAREC country road systems, which demonstrate the greater risk of speed through unforgiving roadsides and low levels of protection from vehicles (photos by S. Job).

In CAREC countries, speeding is also recognized by authorities and in research as a major contributor to serious crashes.[156] Finally, looking at the role of speeding in isolation leaves aside other serious issues with speeds that are too high for safety, but within the legal speed limits, which are commonly higher than what is needed for safety.

These analyses of speed and speed limits in CAREC countries highlight the substantial opportunities that exist in CAREC for saving crash deaths, serious injuries, and economic costs by lowering speed limits and travel speeds. In particular, CAREC countries will benefit from not simply adopting HIC speed limits, and instead by setting speed limits that reflect the greater levels of risk on CAREC roads.

---

[156] C. Wang, C. Xu, and P. Fan. 2020. Effects of Traffic Enforcement Cameras on Macro-Level Traffic Safety: A Spatial Modeling Analysis Considering Interactions with Roadway and Land Use Characteristics. *Accident Analysis & Prevention*. 144. 105659; K. Ibrayev et al. 2019. Analysis of the State of the Road Traffic Safety in the Republic of Kazakhstan. **Наука и техника**. (6). pp. 482–489; J. Demberelsuren. 2016. 474 Road Traffic Injuries and Deaths and Their Risk Factors in Mongolia. *Injury Prevention*. 22. A172.

E. Common Myths About Speed

Myth 1: Higher speed is better for the economy.

Lower speeds are better for the economy overall. Economically ideal speeds for road travel are consistently found to be lower than existing speed limits; road crash costs are huge and even retard long-term economic growth, including in CAREC countries. Everyone pays the cost of high speed, and just a small proportion of companies and people receive the benefits.

The myth that higher speeds are better for the economy persists for two main reasons. First, some economic analyses of higher speeds only consider travel time savings, omitting the critical economic impacts of crash costs, emissions, fuel costs, and vehicle maintenance. Second, the total costs of speed are often overlooked because lobbying by transport companies and other road users is focused on their travel time, while the main costs of crashes and health effects of emissions are borne by society and government.

> *Everyone pays the cost of high speed, and just a small proportion of companies and people receive the benefits.*

Myth 2: Becoming a higher-income country will fix road safety.

In general, HICs do have better road safety records than LMICs. However, within HICs and within LMICs road safety performance varies greatly, showing that some HICs do it badly, and some LMICs do road safety much better than others. It is possible for LMICs to improve their road safety, and lowering travel speeds is the most cost-effective way to do so.

Road safety costs are one of the key retarding factors in the economic growth of LMICs. So, instead of thinking that a country must become high-income first, evidence rather shows that improving road safety first will help it become an HIC.

Myth 3: Higher speed limits solve congestion, and lower speed limits make congestion worse.

Congestion is a significant issue in many major global cities. A common assumption among policymakers and politicians is that increasing speed limits (and thus supposedly speeds) will solve congestion. This assumption misunderstands the relationship of congestion to speed. First, by definition, congestion means that the traffic is not able to reach the speed limit—so higher speed limits will not solve the problem of excessive traffic for the road space available. Second, increasing speeds does not simply mean that more vehicles get through a given location on the road; as speeds increase, drivers should (and generally do) leave longer gaps between themselves and the vehicle in front. Thus, at high speed, vehicles are further apart. Third, speeds are often slowed by slow moving vehicles and stopped vehicles seeking or in the process of parking, dropping passengers, or delivering goods.

Figure 9 shows the theoretical curve relating speed to traffic flow (in green), along with actual data from many locations, showing an excellent fit with the curve (in blue dots). At low levels, as speed increases the traffic flow initially improves, but with further increases in speed, the opposite effect occurs: traffic flow through a specific location is reduced as speeds increase. In higher traffic contexts, if the posted speed is more than the speed at the time, there is little loss in travel time with decreasing the speed limit. At higher operating speeds in free-flow conditions, increasing speeds in net will reduce flow, and thus may increase congestion. Based on this evidence, variable speed limits (including managed freeways) have been used with positive results for both improved safety and reduced congestion.[157] Reducing speed limits as vehicles reach congested conditions results in a smoother flow of traffic, which may be achieved though variable speed limits set to the level of congestion. This produces less "stop/start and slow then accelerate" activity, with subsequent benefits on safety and throughput of vehicles.

---

[157] C. Han et al. 2009. *Best Practice for Variable Speed Limits: Literature Review.* AP-R342/09. Sydney, Australia: Austroads.

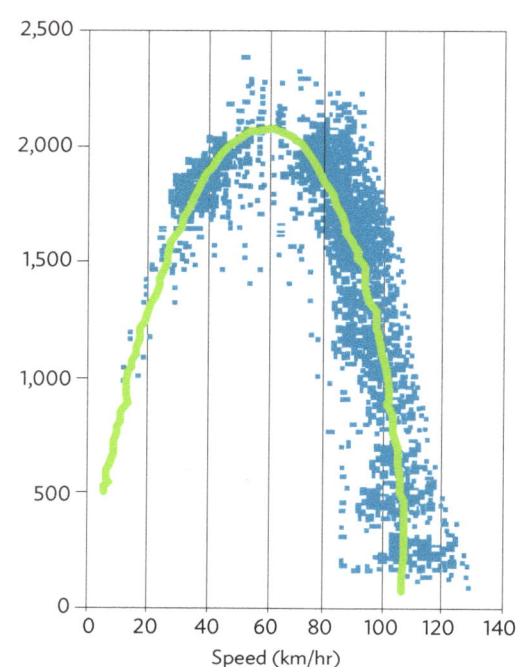

Figure 9: Relationship Between Speed and Traffic Flow

km/hr = kilometer per hour, veh/hr = vehicle per hour.
Note: Two interpretations of this figure are possible. The figure may simply show that as roads become congested and so have less throughput of vehicles, speeds slow down, OR it may be that as speeds are slowed there is less throughput of vehicles. In reality, both mechanisms are at work. The first is clear and requires no further explanation. The second requires understanding that the way most drivers behave is as follows: When traveling at high speed such as 80 km/h, they leave a longer gap between their vehicle and the vehicle in front (ideally around 4 seconds for safety, though on average drivers may be a little below this), but at 50 km/h the gap can be less (ideally around 3 seconds for safety, though again often drivers are a little below this), and at 30 km/h the gap may be a bit less again. The consequence of this is that in each lane at 80 km/h one vehicle goes past a given point around every 4 seconds, but at 50 km/h a vehicle can go through around every 3 seconds, and so on. Thus, slower speeds allow more vehicles to pass through.
Source: R.F.S. Job and L.W. Mbugua. 2020. *Road Crash Trauma, Climate Change, Pollution and the Total Costs of Speed: Six Graphs that Tell the Story*. GRSF Note 2020.1. Washington DC: World Bank. Figure was based on Organisation for Economic Co-operation and Development. 2006. *Speed Management*. Report of the Transport Research Center, ECMT Paris.

Myth 4: Improving driver skill and more training will fix the speed problem.

As described earlier in this module, speed is the most important determinant of crash severity and a major determinant of crash occurrence as well. As described in Appendix 2, the evidence shows that training drivers in car handling skills does not improve road safety and often does the opposite, with crashes increasing after training.

Myth 5: Germany has safe roads with unlimited speeds.

Germany is often cited as an example of road safety success without managing speed. This is quite misleading.

The motorway system in Germany (the Autobahn) is built to high safety standards. Although at one time all Germany's motorways famously had no speed limit, speed management has for some years been a vital part of Germany's road safety approach and a key reason for Germany's road safety improvements. Germany's approach to speed management is quite strict. In response to the number of serious crashes and deaths occurring on its motorways, German authorities reacted by putting speed limits on almost half of them including installing almost 5,000 speed cameras; a low enforcement tolerance, with 3 km/h over the speed limit being a punishable offense; a 50 km/h maximum urban speed limit (footnote 5); and a 30 km/h limits in many city centers and residential areas.[158]

However, Germany is still significantly behind the road safety records of the best-performing countries in Europe (Sweden, the Netherlands, and Norway), which have speed limits on all their streets and roads, including motorways. Due to extreme speeds and no speed limits on some motorways, despite being the best engineered roads in Europe, Germany's motorways are less safe than those of many similar countries in Europe; the motorways of Denmark, France, Ireland, the Netherlands, Switzerland, and the UK, all show better safety records.[159]

---

[158] ETSC. 2015. Germany Unblocks 30km/h Zones. 17 April.
[159] ETSB. 2008. *German Autobahn*: The Speed Limit Debate. Speed Factsheet 01-08.

Myth 6: Speed enforcement is mainly for revenue raising.

Speed is critical to road safety, and speed enforcement works for road safety, not simply to collect revenue. Many jurisdictions, such as El Salvador and some states in Australia, have in fact implemented policies to pass all speed camera fine revenue back to use for road safety programs, so that the revenue is not used by the government for other purposes.

Myth 7: High levels of motorization are key to economic development.

The perception that high levels of motorization are needed for economic development arises from comparisons of HICs with more motorization and low-income countries with less motorization. However, correlation is not proof that high levels of motorization help with the economy. This relationship can also be explained as HICs being able to afford more motorization, rather that motorization causing higher incomes.

Some of the wealthiest countries do not have the highest motorization rates and have designed their cities to rely on mass public transport, not personal motorized travel. For example, the largest metropolis on earth, Tokyo, could not function on private motor transport and relies on expansive use of the metro system for commuting. Japan also relies on fast trains for intercity transport, and perhaps it is no coincidence that Japan is a major global economy and has one of the longest life expectancies of any country.[160]

Thus, we should not assume that more motorization leads to better economic growth, and based on the evidence for the extensive costs of increasing motorization (as presented in this module) this seems most unlikely. Mass transit development is a healthier, less space consuming, and more cost-effective way to develop transport in cities.

Myth 8: I am a good driver so I am safe to speed.

Drivers who have more car handling skill have more, not fewer, crashes. Drivers who are more confident of their driving take more risks, and this leads to more crashes.

Myth 9: Mostly it is the extreme speeders who have serious crashes.

Each instance of extreme speeding does have dramatically more risk of a serious crash than what is commonly seen as low-level speeding. For example, Nilsson's finding of a 4% increase in fatal crash risk for each 1% increase in speed means that at 5 km/h above an 80 km/h speed limit, the risk of a fatal crash is elevated by 25%. At 30 km/h above the speed limit however risk is elevated by 150%—about 6 times the risk. However, if there are six instances of "minor" speed for each instance of extreme speeding, then the low-level speeding in total will contribute to as many fatal crashes as the extreme speeding in total. In most places, many more than six times as many people are speeding by 5 km/h than speeding by 30 km/h, meaning that low-level speeding contributes in fact to more deaths and serious injuries than the extreme speeding. For example, analysis based on increased risk per instance and number of instances shows that supposed "minor" speeding is killing more people than the rarer extreme speeding. In Australia, such analysis showed that 67% of speeding deaths are caused by people speeding by 1 km/h to 10 km/h above the limit, while only 3% were caused by the rare drivers speeding by 30 km/h or more over the limit.[161]

Thus, a focus on extreme speeding will only reduce a small percentage of speeding-related deaths. The exact percentage will vary from country to country, depending on the percentages of drivers speeding by each amount.[162]

---

[160] S. Tokudome, S. Hashimoto, and A. Igata. 2016. Life Expectancy and Healthy Life Expectancy of Japan: The Fastest Graying Society in the World. *BMC Research Notes*. 9 (1). pp. 1–6.

[161] A. Gavin et al. 2010. Is a Focus on Low Level Speeding Justified? Objective Determination of the Relative Contributions of Low and High Level Speeding to the Road Toll. In Proceedings of Australasian Road Safety Research, Policing and Education Conference. Canberra.

[162] A. Gavin et al. 2011. *Creation and Validation of a Tool to Measure the Real Population Risk of Speeding.* In Proceedings of the 2011 Australasian Road Safety Research, Policing and Education Conference.

Myth 10: Safer vehicles and roads will fix speed so we do not need safe speeds.

Safer roads and safer vehicles do help road safety. However, unless speeds are managed as well, the level of safety required of roads and vehicles will be prohibitively expensive, and the design of cities would require complete separation of cars and vulnerable road users, with many overhead footbridges along with many other visual and functional movement problems.

Myth 11: Lower speed limits will lead to much slower journeys.

In light of the effects of higher speed on congestion and the role of many factors (e.g., intersections, crossings, other slow vehicles), some studies have reported that lower speed limits can reduce travel times in urban areas.[163] Furthermore, a faster journey yields an erroneously perceived time gain, or saving, far in excess of the objective time gain, which is in fact only marginal, especially for shorter trips.[164] Even a simple calculation of the difference in time taken from distance and speed will over-estimate the real time difference because for some of the journey vehicles are slowed by other vehicles, curves, turns, intersections and so on. Thus, if a vehicle is forced to slow to 60 km/h for 30% of a journey, then lowering the speed limit from 90 km/h to 70 km/h will not change the speed of this 30% of the journey. Finally, where a series of signalized points exist along a road, appropriate coordination of these signals can help to manage speeds, and this can be especially helpful if drivers understand that driving at a higher speed simply results in stopping for longer at the next signal.

Myth 12: The evidence on the critical role of speed comes from high-income countries, so does not apply in low- and middle-income countries.

Most of the evidence does come from HICs. However, because the laws of physics apply everywhere, and humans make mistakes everywhere, the same effects of speed will occur everywhere. However, the effects of speed can produce different results. For example, in a city with few pedestrians and mostly car-to-car crashes, many instances of speeding at 50 km/h in a 40 km/h zone will not result in many deaths because even at 50 km/h most crashes are survivable. But the same speeding in a city with many pedestrians or motorcycles will cause many deaths, because at 50 km/h most pedestrians or motorcycle riders will not survive. Thus, speeding in low-income countries produces worse road safety outcomes than in HICs.

The evidence directly supports this. One study found that the speed factor alone accounted for more than 50% of all road traffic crashes in Ghana.[165] Assessment of the benefits of reducing speeds found huge safety improvements in LMICs (footnote 13), and the BCRs for speed-managing interventions are higher in LMICs than in HICs.[166]

Myth 13: Individual road users are responsible for their own safety and the safety of others, rather than the road system and its speeds.

The safe system approach is delivering dramatic successes in road safety by accepting that humans will inevitably make mistakes, and the road system needs to protect people from death and disability even when such mistakes are made. Placing the responsibility back on to road users means that we are accepting a system in which people can receive a death penalty for a momentary lapse of concentration or a slight misjudgment. This is not accepted in any other government-managed environment.

---

[163] J. Archer et al. 2008. The Impact of Lowered Speed Limits in Urban and Metropolitan Areas. Report #276. Monash University Accident Research Center.
[164] European Commission. 2019. Mobility and Transport. Road Safety.
[165] F. K. Afukaar. 2003. Speed Control in Developing Countries: Issues, Challenges and Opportunities in Reducing Road Traffic Injuries. Injury Control and Safety Promotion. 10 (1–2). pp. 77–81.
[166] R. F. S. Job and L. W. Mbugua. 2020. Road Crash Trauma, Climate Change, Pollution and the Total Costs of Speed: Six Graphs That Tell the Story. GRSF Note 2020.1. Washington DC: Global Road Safety Facility, World Bank.

F. Recommendations

Based on the evidence, the following recommendations are made:

- Employ the information in this manual to appreciate, promote, and explain the need for speed management, and dispel any myths, which are cited as reasons for inaction or weak action on speed management.
- Reducing speeds must be a top priority in improving road safety. Reducing speeds would deliver over half the UN target of a 50% reduction in deaths by road crashes and accidents by 2030. Supposedly faster options, such as education, are ineffective.
- Speed data are in themselves a vital tool for road safety and the management of speed. Thus, on-road (not self-reported) surveys of travel are vitally important for road safety management.
- International Road Assessment Programme (iRAP) tools such as the iRAP Star Rating Demonstrator are useful for estimating the impact of speed on serious crashes. This is a free, evidence-based way of quickly estimating the impact of safety on different speed scenarios and designs. See: https://demonstrator.vida.irap.org/
- Use the tool provided by Gavin et al.[167] and data on speeds of travel in the relevant country to calculate the proportion of deaths caused by extreme speeding and by low-level speeding to dispel the myth that extreme speeders are the main issue.
- For policymakers and for economic appraisals of speeds by governments and funders, speed reduction should be included as a policy option for improving overall economic growth.
- Road safety actions on speed should be based on evidence that they work to reduce crashes, injuries, and/or deaths, not on apparent common sense.
- Driver training programs (especially skills based, skid control, and all off-road courses) do not improve road safety and often cause an increase in crash rates. These should be avoided, and proponents of "new" types of training should not be considered. Supposed evidence for success, such as that people feel safer or have more skill after the course, should be considered as evidence for road safety failure because these results are the source of increased overconfidence and risk-taking (see Module IV). Only courses shown through independent, well-controlled evaluation to reduce subsequent crashes should be prioritized.
- Providing learner drivers with many hours of on-road supervised experience (with supervision by a driver with multiple years of experience) before solo driving is allowed, rather than skills training, is the only "training" shown to improve subsequent road safety. This is recommended for adoption by licensing agencies.
- Road safety agencies and departments of education must appreciate that school-based education on road safety (like school-based driver training) does not improve road safety. Road safety resources should not be spent on it. However, it is often politically impossible to stop such training. If well-meaning volunteer groups, ambulance, or police are providing road safety education this should be replaced with road safety being included in the school curriculum and taught by teachers who understand the learning needs of the children.
- Government regulation to limit advertising (as exists in various countries) that promotes speed is recommended to help to reduce support for high speed.
- High-fear campaigns and messages are popular and show good results in audience testing because they are seen as impactful, yet the evidence shows that these are ineffective in changing on-road behavior and improving road safety, especially compared with campaigns and advertising based on enforcement. (See Module IV for an explanation of why this is the case.)
- For road authorities, engineers, planners, and senior decision-makers: Increasing speeds increases crashes and increases crash severity. If speeds must be increased (noting that this is often mistakenly understood to improve the economy) then for safety any speed increase must be accompanied by real safety treatments to reverse the increased crash risk—crash barriers, speed humps, raised crossing, and so on, depending on the nature of the road and its users.
- For road authorities, engineers, and road maintenance managers—improving road surfaces for smoother driving by fixing bumps and rough surfaces should not be seen as a road safety treatment. These treatments increase speeds and thus increase serious crashes, and this increase far

---

[167] A. Gavin, E. Walker, R. Fernandes, A. Graham, R.F.S. Job, and J. Sergeant. 2011. Creation and validation of a tool to measure the real population risk of speeding. In Proceedings of the 2011 Australasian Road Safety Research, Policing and Education Conference.

outweighs any safety benefits of removing these road surface issues. Where such an intervention is planned, for safety it must be accompanied by other treatments to reverse the increased safety risk, such as crash barriers, speed humps, or raised crossings, depending on the nature of the road and its users.

- Suggestions to adopt any of the above failing (at worst harmful to road safety, or at best ineffective) options should be strongly resisted based on the evidence presented here, which can be adopted as the basis of the argument. It is important to present alternative effective actions to decision-makers in this process.

- Based on the logic and evidence that police-based crash data miss many speeding crashes, countries should not rely on data to estimate the extent of their speeding problem in relation to serious crashes. Instead, this should be discussed with police, and their correction factor (and evidence for it)[168] could be applied to provide a more informative estimate of the real role of speeding in fatal and serious crashes for the country, state, province, or city.

---

[168] R. F. S. Job and C. Brodie. 2022. Understanding the Role of Speeding and Speed in Serious Crash Trauma: A Case Study of New Zealand. *Journal of Road Safety*. 33 (1). pp. 5–25

Appendix 1: Examples of Private Sector Campaigns Encouraging Speed

Community and decision-maker views of some risky on-road behaviors remain positive, especially surrounding speeding.[1] One set of reasons for this relates to the road transport system being in significant part provided by the private sector, along with their deliberate and profound influence on risky on-road behavior, their actions to directly limit political will and management of behaviors such as speeding, and road transport itself.

Examples include:

- Industries pay scientists, thus creating bias in commentaries and scientific research.[2] Major oil and/or fuel companies have funded, shaped, and promoted the claim that climate change is not real,[3] have created misunderstandings relating to climate change,[4] and succeeded in pushing some governments to retreat from climate change agreements.[5] This misinformation reduces the value of policies to shift away from road transport to more climate-friendly transport options.
- Vehicle manufacturers are mixed in their contributions to safety, adding some safety technology to vehicles (although many safety contributions must be forced on the industry by the New Car Assessment Program,[6] generating market forces for safety and by government regulation). Various car makers still manufacture vehicles to a lower safety standard for low- and middle-income country markets than for the same vehicle models sold in high-income countries. Car and motorcycle manufacturers are especially unhelpful on speed. Many continue to:

    » advertise their cars or motorcycles based on speed, power, and acceleration, which are presented as exciting, sexy, macho, and fun;[7]
    » promote speed capability through technologies that make cars more comfortable at high speed;[8]
    » universally manufacture vehicles capable of speeds greatly in excess of the maximum speed limits in most countries into which they are sold;
    » install speedometers that show extremely high speeds and reduce the visual size of speed differences around typical speed limits;
    » resist implementation of important technologies that have been available for years to help manage speed (speed governing at a maximum speed, or with sensitivity to speed limits, via intelligent speed adaptation). Instead, voluntary or advisory intelligent speed adaptation, which informs the driver but does not limit speeds, is available in some vehicles.

---

[1] C. Hydén. 2020. Speed in a High-Speed Society. *International Journal of Injury Control and Safety Promotion.* 27 (1). pp. 44–50; and L. Mooren. R. Grzebieta, and S. Job. 2013. *Speed: The Biggest and Most Contested Road Killer.* Proceedings of the Australasian College of Road Safety Conference, A Safe System: The Road Safety Discussion. October. Adelaide.

[2] S. Greenhalgh. 2021. Inside ILSI: How Coca-Cola, Working through Its Scientific Nonprofit, Created a Global Science of Exercise for Obesity and Got It Embedded in Chinese Policy (1995–2015). *Journal of Health Politics, Policy and Law.* 46 (2). pp. 235–276; and C. A. Mebane et al. 2019. Scientific Integrity Issues in Environmental Toxicology and Chemistry: Improving Research Reproducibility, Credibility, and Transparency. Integrated Environmental Assessment and Management. 15 (3). pp. 320–344.

[3] M. Grasso. 2019. Oily Politics: A Critical Assessment of the Oil and Gas Industry's Contribution to Climate Change. *Energy Research & Social Science.* 50. pp. 106–115.

[4] G. Supran and N. Oreskes. 2021. Rhetoric and Frame Analysis of ExxonMobil's Climate Change Communications. *One Earth.* 4 (5). pp. 696–719.

[5] A. J. Hoffman. 2005. Climate Change Strategy: The Business Logic Behind Voluntary Greenhouse Gas Reductions. *California Management Review.* 47 (3). pp. 21–46.

[6] The New Car Assessment Program (ANCAP) is a car safety assessment program based on crash testing. Results are promoted to the public.

[7] These views of speed and power remain for many, as shown in this article and responses to it: I. Bober. 2017. Performance Cars are Pointless... In this Country? Practical Motoring. May 12; and R. Green. 2020. Audi Australia Sets Pulses Racing in 'Raised by Racecars' R/RS Campaign via the Monkeys. *Campaign Brief.* August 7.

[8] Mercedes-Benz. Magic Body Control. S-Class. 2014. Video. 1:52.

- Many private sector media outlets promote speed and criticize its regulation;[9] and
- Many trucking/logistics companies advocate for governments to resist lowering speed limits and push for high speeds, from which they appear to reap economic benefits. This advocacy fails to understand the net costs of speed to societies, and limits political will to reduce speeds and to treat speeding more seriously.[10] The external costs of road transport (which includes the costs of high speed such as crashes, deaths, and injuries, as well as other costs) are generally neglected in considerations of speed management policy.[11] These major costs of speed are generally suffered by individual victims and societies more broadly, and their costs are paid by governments. Thus, road transport and logistics companies reap the economic benefits of higher speeds, while the rest of society pays the costs, which greatly exceed the economic benefits.[12]

A related set of other social and psychological factors promote speed, and thus resistance to its management. Faster is seen as better: Races are part of almost all our childhoods, as well as being spectator sports won through speed, and there is no fundamental sense to a competition on who is the slowest. Usain Bolt is a household name because he was the fastest, as was Michael Schumacher in Formula One cars. No one is a household name because they are the safest. Faster is also misunderstood as being better for the economy.

Adding to all this promotion of speed and perhaps in part because of this promotion, risk-taking including speeding has strong positive value for young drivers,[13] who are at greatest risk of speeding crashes.[14] The problem is compounded by misjudgment of risk.

---

[9] For example, P. Litras, and S. Spits. 2010. Mark Webber Attacks 'Nanny State. *Sydney Morning Herald*. March 29; and S. Meredith. 2017. There's a Speed Camera That's Generating Enough Money to Rival the Average Business. *CNBC European News*. 4 January.

[10] This is often successful. See R. F. Job. 2018. Perspective on Road Safety: Safe Speeds Part 1: Political Decisions and the Limited Adoption of Speed Management for Road Safety. *Journal of the Australasian College of Road Safety*. 29 (3). pp. 65.

[11] Z. Raza, M. Svanberg, and B. Wiegmans. 2020. Modal Shift from Road Haulage to Short Sea Shipping: A Systematic Literature Review and Research Directions. *Transport Reviews*. 40 (3). pp. 382–406.

[12] See Module 1.

[13] T. Prabhakar, S.H.V. Lee, and R. F. S. Job. 1996. *Risk Taking, Optimism Bias and Risk Utility in Drivers*. In L. St. John, ed. Proceedings of the Road Safety Research and Enforcement Conference. pp.61-68. Sydney, Australia: Roads & Traffic Authority of NSW.

[14] C. Sakashita. 2007. *Comparing Provisional and Unrestricted Licence Holders on Speeding Offences and Crash Rates.* In Proceedings of the Australasian Road Safety Research Policing and Education Conference. Melbourne, Australia. 17–19 October.

Appendix 2: Why Driver and School Education Is Ineffective

A. The Decision Problem and Suggested Solutions

It is common for decision-makers, politicians, and some road safety advocates to resist the quite clear evidence that road safety education, school-based driver training, and skill-based driver training alone do not work to improve road safety. This resistance has many underlying causes:

- the extrapolation of the success of education in so many other areas;
- the common-sense view that this must work; and
- the low cost of this intervention, making it quite appealing.

While none of these arguments dismiss the evidence, it is important to be realistic. In response to this push for road safety education, the broad community popularity of road safety education for young children in schools should be acknowledged, along with the importance of the community seeing the government as concerned to prevent crash deaths and injuries. Support for the continuation of this education can be made with specific refinements:

- Road safety education should be made part of the compulsory school curriculum and be taught by the school teachers who are trained to teach children, and who understand the children's learning needs. It should not be taught by well-meaning volunteers or emergency personnel or police. This is best practice and will minimize costs to road safety organizations.
- Road safety education should include the one area where it may work, which is teachers training children at the roadside about where and how to cross the road. This should be given at around age 8 years, not earlier. Younger children should always be supervised when crossing roads, and training can give the false impression that children who are too young to do so can cross a road safely.
- Government must appreciate that this is not a significant solution for road safety, and evidence-based actions must be funded and adopted as well.
- Government should not be persuaded by any individuals or company claiming to have a version of road safety education that works unless they can demonstrate independently conducted evaluations showing reductions in crashes, deaths, and injuries, not just the usual improved knowledge (with no proof that this will improve safety).
- Avoid this being funded from any road safety budget or by police and promote that the department of education should fund it.

Most critically, the same approach cannot be taken for driver training in schools, because the evidence as briefly reviewed below indicates that this is likely to increase crash risk for those who are trained. This must be prevented from occurring. It is worthwhile to cite the evidence provided here and to explain why this happens (using the explanation of starting driving at a younger age, and thus with less well-developed brain regions to control impulses to take risks, as presented in this appendix).

For driver training more generally, off-road skills-based driver training, such as emergency stopping or skid control training, must be resisted. Instead, refer to the evidence that many hours of on-road supervised experience as a learner driver does reduce subsequent crash rates. Again, provide the psychological understanding of these results based on skills training causing an increase in overconfidence and in risk-taking.

B. Summary of the Evidence

Driver training is repeatedly proven to be ineffective, and often harmful, for road safety in most circumstances. The evidence is as follows:

Driver and motorcycle rider training

- The Cochrane Library has published expert, methodologically rigorous reviews of evidence from many countries that shows no safety benefits of driver training. For example, the review of post-license driver training concluded: "This systematic review provides no evidence that post-license driver education is effective in preventing road traffic injuries or crashes. …. Because of the large number of participants included in the meta-analysis (close to 300,000 for some outcomes) we can exclude, with reasonable precision, the possibility of even modest benefits." The analysis of the evidence also found that: "No one form of [training]… was found to be substantially more effective than another, nor was a significant difference found between advanced driver education [training] and remedial driver education [training]."[1]

- A review of evidence demonstrates increases in crash rates from vehicle handling skills-based training such as skid training.[2] In the United States, drivers given skid training showed an increase in crashes compared with controls;[3] and training caused higher driver violation rates and higher crash rates after training compared with untrained controls.[4]
- For motorbike riding, again the Cochrane Library has published an expert, methodologically rigorous review of the evidence, showing that there is no sound evidence for safety benefits of rider training.[5] In Australia, a motorcycle rider training (coaching) program resulted in an increase in crashes following training compared with controls.[6] Evaluation of many hours of on-road supervised driving practice (instead of skill-based training) was however helpful for safety.[7]
- For school-based driver training, the Cochrane Library conducted an expert, methodologically rigorous review of the evidence, showing that evaluations of school-based driver training produced negative results, concluding as follows: "The results show that driver education leads to early licensing. They provide no evidence that driver education reduces road crash involvement, and suggest that it may lead to a modest but potentially important increase in the proportion of teenagers involved in traffic crashes."[8] A review of evidence concluded: "The consistent findings from these studies have been that high school driver education does not reduce crashes."[9]
- Brain development studies show that the frontal cortex of the human brain (the brain area responsible for inhibiting the impulse to take risks) develops gradually and is the last area to be developed, so is still not at its maximum strength until the ages of 19 to 25 years, varying from individual to individual. Thus, the earlier start to driving means that young people are driving before their brains are ready to do it safely.[10]

No study has yet shown a road safety benefit of school-based road safety education. Evidence presented is usually of improved knowledge, with no evidence that this will lead to improved safety, or is poorly controlled. An exception is an Australian study that included a comparable control group, which found that those trained subsequently had more crashes than the untrained control group.[11] There is one possible exception to this, which should

---

[1] K. Ker et al. 2003. Post-Licence Driver Education for the Prevention of Road Traffic Crashes. Cochrane Database of Systematic Review. Issue 3. Art. No.: CD003734.

[2] R. Elvik et al. 2009. The Handbook of Road Safety Measures.

[3] B. Jones. 1995. The Effectiveness of Skid-Car Training for Teenage Novice Drivers in Oregon. *The Chronicle of American Driver & Traffic Safety Education Association*. 43 (1). pp. 1–8.

[4] Disappointingly, the authors of this evaluation also suggest the possibility of improvement years after training, based on weak evidence on near-misses, not on crash rates. This type of commentary may reflect the ongoing need to believe that this type of training can deliver benefits, despite the evidence to the contrary. J. Mueller, L. Stanley, and K. R. Manlove. 2012. Multi-Stage Novice Defensive Driver Training Program: Does It Create Overconfidence? *Open Journal of Safety Science and Technology*. 2 (4). pp. 133.

[5] K. Kardamanidis et al. 2010. Motorcycle Rider Training for the Prevention of Road Traffic Crashes. The Cochrane Library.

[6] R. Ivers et al. 2016. Does an On-Road Motorcycle Coaching Program Reduce Crashes in Novice Riders? A Randomised Control Trial. *Accident Analysis & Prevention*. 86. pp. 40–46.

[7] N. P. Gregersen. 2003. Accident Involvement Among Learner Drivers—An Analysis of the Consequences of Supervised Practice. *Accident Analysis & Prevention*. 35 (5). pp. 725–730.

[8] Roberts IG, Kwan I. 2001. School-Based Driver Education for the Prevention of Traffic Crashes. *Cochrane Database of Systematic Reviews*. Issue 3.

[9] B. O'Neill. 2020. *Driver Education: How Effective? International Journal of Injury Control and Safety Promotion*. 27:1. pp. 61–68. DOI: 10.1080/17457300.2019.1694042

[10] S. B. Johnson and V. C. Jones. 2011. Adolescent Development and Risk of Injury: Using Developmental Science to Improve Interventions. *Injury Prevention*. 17 (1). pp. 50–54; and B. J. Casey, R. M. Jones, and T. A. Hare. 2008. The Adolescent Brain. *Annals of the New York Academy of Sciences*. 1124. pp. 111–126.

[11] J. B. Carlin, P. Taylor, and T. Nolan. 1998. School Based Bicycle Safety Education and Bicycle Injuries in Children: A Case-Control Study. *Injury Prevention*. 4 (1). pp. 22–27.

be considered: taking children to the roadside and training them in how and where to cross the road, which does improve road crossing behavior. In Australia, training children in how and where to cross the road improved their subsequent road crossing behavior.[12] The Cochrane Library review of this area found that studies did show apparent improvements in behavior from the training, but also found that there was no proof that this change would last or reduce crash risk.[13]

---

[12] J. Oxley et al. 2008. Teaching Young Children to Cross Roads Safely. *Ann Adv Automot Med.* 52. pp. 215–23.

[13] O. Duperrex, I. Roberts, and F. Bunn. 2002. Safety Education of Pedestrians for Injury Prevention. *The Cochrane Library*.